Heart
of the
Storm

...a journey toward hope

Jill H. Loera

Spring Mill Publishing

Sharpsburg, Maryland USA

For my wonderful husband, Al,
amazing son, Alfie,

and

to my precious daughter, Lana, for
teaching me about what's important.

Heart of the Storm
...a journey toward hope

by Jill H. Loera
Copyright © 2018 by Jill H. Loera

ISBN: 9781728733845

Published by
SPRING MILL PUBLISHING
Sharpsburg, Maryland 21782 USA

Graphics and Layout by Marianne Maust Aguilar

Table of Contents

Heart

of the

Storm

...a journey toward hope

Jill H. Loera

Heart of the Storm is an honest and compelling book that follows the journey of the author, Jill Loera, and her family, through the heart-wrenching physical trials that her daughter Lana went through. Through this book, Jill also gives the reader a look into her own journey from childhood, through the agony of painful valleys, until both she and her family emerge on the other side.

Readers will find, even as I did, that this book is a signpost directing them to the One who will never leave them and who has answers and help when we need it most.

Pastor Elver Mendenhall
Rancho Christian Center
Rancho Cucamonga, CA

My heart is heavy and I long for shelter from the storm which rages all around me. The weight of this world is overwhelming and it hurts to breathe.

"SAVE me, O God!
For the waters have come up to my neck.
I sink in deep mire, where there is
no standing;
I have come into deep waters,
where the floods
overflow me."
- Psalm 69:1-2

"From the end of the earth I will cry to You,
When my heart is overwhelmed;
Lead me to the rock that is higher than I.
For You have been a shelter for me,
A strong tower from the enemy.
I will abide in Your tabernacle forever;
I will trust in the shelter of Your wings."
- Psalm 61:1-4

Those Snowy Days

I was born in New York. It was a fun upbringing, especially during the winter season when it snowed. I used to watch as the beautiful white snow covered our backyard. AND, the more it snowed, the more likely we were to have the day off from school. All of us kids on the block would stand outside and listen for the sound of the gong which meant that school would be canceled. It also meant that my brother, Devin and I could play in the snow ALL DAY while having snowball fights, building snowmen, and hanging out in the igloo (built by my dad).

When our gloves became so drenched that we could no longer feel our fingers, my mom would leave dry gloves for us on the porch by the back door. She would also keep our cups filled with delicious hot chocolate. Mom went back and forth from the house to the porch and from the porch to the house throughout the day.

We were good friends with our neighbors Marilyn, Dick, and their kids, Chuck and Helene. Sometimes the snow was so high that it covered the gate separating our backyards, so, we would climb over the snow to get to each other's yards. Helene was so tiny that we would often lose her in the snow.

I loved our house, especially because it had the coolest room ever - a basement - which my brother and I turned into a combination classroom and party room. We had a chalkboard and a table that we used as a desk; I was the teacher and Devin was the student. I would take a thick red marker and correct whatever mistakes I felt he made on his papers. As Devin's "teacher," I was smart and powerful (even though he was really the smarter one!).

The focus of our "party room" was a forty dollar "state of the art" record player which would play songs from our vinyl "45" records. I especially remember dancing with my cousin, Patti, to songs like: "Sugar Sugar," "Build Me Up Buttercup," and others. *For anyone under the age of fifty who is reading this, you may need to ask an older person what a "45 record" is.*

I Am Jewish

When I was young, I could feel the presence of God and knew that He was watching over me. I was born Jewish. Although my family and I weren't involved in religious activities on a regular basis, we celebrated Hanukah, Rosh Hashanah, Yom Kippur, Passover, and attended temple for Bar Mitzvahs and funerals.

The "High Holidays" (Rosh Hashanah and Yom Kippur) were especially important to my grandparents - in fact, every year on Yom Kippur, my grandmother would [1]fast (into her nineties!) in order to please God and to follow the tradition of her parents.

Even though I went along with these events, I was confused. I didn't understand how God fit into our lives and believed that if he were truly "God," then he would show me personally who he was, why he was here, and what he had in store for my life.

About Family

My parents were very much in love for all forty-eight years of their married life. My dad worked for the same company for over thirty years as a salesman and district manager. To this day, he is still a loyal and devoted gentleman who has been blessed with many gifts. He has a lively personality, great sense of humor; is a proficient singer, writer, director and self-taught harmonica player; and is loved by many *(especially me!)*.

My mom was highly intelligent and put her whole heart into everything she did. She earned her Master's Degree in audiology and became an audiologist at twenty years of age. While we were young, my mom worked as a teacher for children who were learning to speak English. She developed educational programs which are still being implemented today. In later years, I followed some of my mom's lessons while schooling my daughter.

My parents were so devoted to each other that I often felt left out. Especially throughout the teenage years, I was starving for attention and wanted so badly to please them. I felt as though I could never live up to their expectations and could never be worthy of their love.

I longed to spend quality time with mom, but she always seemed pre-occupied with my dad or the general busyness of life. My friends would often talk about having lunch or going to the movies with their mom. My mom and I would go shopping together, but it was painful for me to try on clothes. I didn't like what I saw in the mirror. At the time, I didn't know what to do with the pain and rejection that I continually felt, so I spent many years rebelling against my parents.

Years later, I discovered a redeeming and forgiving love that brought me to the realization that my parents did the best they could while providing me with many wonderful life lessons which I will always be grateful for.

When we were little, I was crazy about my brother, Devin, but as I got older, I decided that he was annoying and that I wasn't going to treat him kindly. In fact, it was a nosebleed which caused me to change my ways. On this particular day, our neighbor Marilyn was in charge because our mother wasn't home. My brother rushed over to me with blood dripping profusely from his nose. I was terrified and panicked: *"He's going to die!"* Hysterically, I ran to Marilyn,

"Do something, Devin is bleeding!" Marilyn knew what to do and after a few minutes, which seemed like a lifetime, the blood stopped. From then on, I was grateful to have a brother.

Still, during the "troubled teen" years, Devin seemed to be the only available outlet on whom to take out my frustrations and problems. So, I would call him names and say cruel things to him. I would love to live that part of my life over and to do things differently, but we all know that this isn't possible.

Devin, if you're reading this, I apologize to you again, and want you to know that I'm so glad that, in spite of me, you are a wonderful man and a great brother!

Devin sort of got back at me when, one day, while I was making fun of him, he hit me over the head with his guitar. I yelled out, "Mom, Devin hit me over the head with the guitar." My parents were laughing hysterically, because what my brother and I didn't know is that while we were fighting, my mom had said to my dad, "He should hit her over the head with his guitar." *By the way, years later that same guitar had to be tossed because my cat Sammi puked in it!*

I had a special relationship with both sets of grandparents who were huge parts of my childhood and brought much joy and love into my life. To this day, I miss that unconditional love!

Nana Lylla, my dad's mother, was a funny lady *(my dad must have gotten his sense of humor from her!)*. One day when my grandmother came over to visit, I said, "Nana, your hair looks funny." She replied, "I burned the front of my wig, so I'm wearing it backwards."

She would give her husband, Papa Jack, the same birthday card each year - and each year he would say, "That's very nice, Lylla." One time, Nana was chewing "Chiclets" (candy-coated chewing gum that was popular in those days). Papa Jack saw that she had gum and said, "Lylla, give me a couple of those Chiclets," to which she replied, "Here" and placed her dentures in his hand instead. When he realized that she had given him her teeth, he said, "That woman is trying to kill me!"

For many years, Nana Lylla wore a beautiful ring which held some diamonds. After she passed away, we took the ring to the jeweler to have it cleaned and appraised. While anxiously waiting to learn of the ring's value, we watched as the jeweler removed pieces of tin foil, one by one, which were in the place where the diamonds used to be. The diamonds had either fallen out or Nana had sold them and replaced them with foil, nevertheless, after all this time, we discovered that we had been "foiled!"

Nana was an excellent cook. She loved cooking for the family and we loved eating her food. In my grandparents' home, there was a ledge leading to the kitchen, which Nana often stumbled over. One time, as she was carrying a bowl of her delicious homemade Matzo Ball soup to her husband, she tripped - the soup landed in my Uncle Shelly's lap, and the knife - which was in her other hand - stabbed the wall.

Nana would often ask me to play her favorite song on the record player - "I Can't Help Falling in Love" by Al Martino. Even though the song didn't mean anything to me back then (now I love it), I am so glad that I played it for her every time. In later years, Nana would come to see us by bus while carrying cooked food (which many times leaked through the containers and through the bags). When the food finally made it to us, it was always tasty, full of love, and worth the wait. Nana Lylla was a special lady who I loved dearly and I knew that someday, I would name my daughter after her.

At every opportunity, we would spend time with my dad's brother, Uncle Shelly, (who sadly passed away in March of 2018), his wife, Aunt Louise, and their daughters,

Melissa and Patti. Looking back on my life, Patti has always been there for me - like a best friend who is also my cousin. Patti and I used to play "dress up" with clothes from Nana Lylla and Papa Jack's closet. We would provide the evening's entertainment by performing fashion shows and commercials for the family. We thought we were extra talented, but I believe that the family put up with us because we were having such a great time.

As children, Cousin Patti and I would look for people to annoy. We would do whatever we could to irritate Patti's sister, Melissa, along with my brother. We were stinkers! BUT, we had fun! *I'm sorry Melissa and Devin - I hope that my actions caused you no permanent damage!*

At my Aunt Louise and Uncle Shelly's fortieth anniversary celebration, Patti and I accidentally walked into the "men's room" and realized, to our horror, that we had entered the wrong room. The family burst into laughter, as they had seen the whole thing. *Boy, were we embarrassed!*

One time, Aunt Louise and Uncle Shelly took Patti and me to dinner at a Chinese restaurant. I was ultra shy and uncomfortable in social situations. Plus, to make matters more difficult, I hadn't seen my relatives in over a year. When ordering our food, Uncle Shelly spoke with a Chinese accent and referred to fried rice as "flied lice." We had a big laugh and from that point on, I was at ease and had a great time.

My mom's parents, Nana Dorothy and Papa Sol, were very involved in our lives. Papa Sol was a kind man who deeply loved his family. He had a special place in his heart for children, especially me! He was in the eye glass business which could have been more successful had he not provided free glasses to anyone who claimed to have a need. *I said he was "kind" - maybe too kind?*

In his later years, Papa Sol became ill and resided in a nursing home. Nana and my mom visited him every day. On Sundays, my dad took Papa to our home so that he could spend the day with us. Whenever I saw him in the nursing home, he was so excited to see me. This was hard because I wasn't able to visit as often as I would have liked and it became harder to leave each time. *I loved him so much!*

After Papa Sol passed away, and until her death at ninety-seven, Nana Dorothy and I became especially close. We talked often - sometimes up to three times a day. Even though we lived miles apart, every morning at ten o'clock, we would talk on the phone as we watched "The Price Is Right" together.

One of the highlights of our relationship was when Nana came with me to a "Wheel of Fortune" audition (I almost made it to the show). The producers were drawn to her and allowed her to remain with me during the entire audition process. She was so excited to be a part of this, and so was I. In later years when I was schooling my kids, she would ask for a schedule in order to follow what we were doing each day.

Nana's son, my Uncle Larry, and cousins, Sheri and Tod, would sometimes spend the night at our house. One New Year's Eve when we were young, we were allowed to stay up, for the first time, past midnight. *We made it, but we were sure tired!*

Bar Mitzvah with family - 1968

My Cat Sammi

My brother and I wanted to have a cat, so my parents took us to the pet store. There were three cats to choose from. My dad said that we could either have the black cat and yellow cat or we could have the gray cat. The first time I picked up the gray cat, she climbed up and down my back. We instantly fell in love with this energetic and adorable animal.

Samantha (Sammi) became my baby. One day, a lady came to our door to tell us that she had just hit a gray cat with her car. My greatest fear came true - Sammi had been severely injured! We rushed her to the vet who said that Sammi had lost sixty-five percent of her blood and that her only chance for survival would be to eat. I followed Sammi around with baby food and a spoon and begged God: "If you're real, you'll save my cat." Sammi lived to be seventeen years old and, from that point on, I was sure that God existed!

Let me tell you a bit about this highly intelligent and creative animal. Sammi didn't like it when we left her alone, so, often while we were gone, she would scurry through my clothing cabinet (which was close to the floor) and carry (in her mouth) my underwear and leave them in a pile in the middle of the living room. She was trying to let us know that this is what we can expect when we leave her alone to guard "her" house.

In those days, we had manual typewriters. To get to the next line of the document, you would push the "arm" of the machine which would make a bell-type sound. Sammi would watch and when we weren't looking, she would push the arm with her paw, sometimes to the point of knocking over the typewriter. *I think she liked the sound of the bell!*

Sammi would do just about anything for attention - and attention she would get!

Tears to Pioneers

Moving to California sounded exciting to me, particularly because our new home was going to have a swimming pool. My mom could no longer tolerate New York's intense cold and my dad was offered a transfer to California, so, when I was ten and a half, my family and I moved from New York to California.

Saying "good-bye" to my grandparents at the airport was one of the most gut-wrenching experiences of my life. I will never forget watching Nana Dorothy and Papa Sol cry uncontrollably because they didn't know when they would see us again. We had been together at least once a week throughout my life, and now were about to be separated. Later, Nana Dorothy told me that they had been so devastated that they had wanted to die.

My grandparents had always been there and had always loved me no matter what mistakes I made. One time, I showed up at my Nana Lylla's house with a suitcase and told her that I didn't want to go home. Through the tears, she said that she was sorry but she had to call my dad (her son) so that he could pick me up.

Now, since we were over three thousand miles away, I would no longer be able to feel their touch and experience the love which always penetrated from their faces when they looked at me. We would talk on the phone (no Skype or Face Time back then), but calls were expensive in those days, so even our time on the phone had to be limited. We recorded messages (and even songs) on tapes and sent the cassettes to them, but this didn't come close to us being together.

I really, really, really missed my grandparents!

It took a year, but finally Nana Dorothy and Papa Sol came out for a visit. It was great to see them, but oh so hard to let them go again.

As it turned out, years later, both sides of the family - and even our next door neighbors - moved from New York to California. To this day, we are still considered "the pioneers of the family!"

Challenges in California

My first year in California was difficult. I was almost eleven years old and about to enter the sixth grade. It was a new school, new home, new neighborhood, new people - and a new life. I was shy and felt completely alone and out of place. I had no friends and missed my grandparents and the rest of the family.

To make matters worse, I had a strong New York accent. I didn't want to give my peers a reason to poke fun, so I decided that the accent had to go. Within a week, I sounded like every other "Californian."

I thought that losing the accent would help, but I was still teased and too humiliated to talk to anyone about it. Often, a girl named Leslie would chase me home and scare me into thinking that she was going to beat me up.

One time I called my mom from the payphone *(no cell phones back then)* while a girl was kicking the door and yelling for me to hurry. I couldn't stop crying. My mom kept asking, "What's wrong?" but I was too embarrassed to let her know what was happening, so I told her that everything was fine.

When I made it home from school each day, I found refuge in my pink and purple coolest girl's bedroom ever! I would lie on my back and stretch out my hands to God and imagine Him holding my hands.

This passage from the Bible shows that God heard my cries all of those years ago:

> [2]*"But You, O LORD, are a shield around me,*
> *My glory and the One who lifts up my head.*
> *I cried to the LORD with my voice,*
> *and He heard me from His holy hill."*

> [3]*"Hear the voice of my supplications*
> *When I cry to you,*
> *When I lift up my hands toward Your*
> *holy sanctuary."*

Teenage Years

From thirteen to fifteen, depression set in. I felt worthless - not good enough - not smart enough - not funny enough - just not enough. I was constantly getting into trouble: cutting classes, cheating on tests, hanging out with the wrong crowd, acting up in class, and being rebellious toward my parents. Although I tried to commit suicide a few times, I knew that I wouldn't really go through with it. I just wanted attention.

During my "class clown" phase, I gave my high school English teacher, Mrs. Ker, such a hard time that years later when she found out that my brother, Devin, was in her class, her face turned white. Devin, thank goodness, was nothing like me, and our teacher seemed to recover! *I would love the opportunity to apologize to Mrs. Ker today.*

When the Dean of Girls, Carol Gorton, called my parents into her office for the second time, Mrs. Gorton told my parents that if she contacted them again, it would be to inform them that I had been expelled.

Falling in Love

At fifteen, I fell in love - with the world of acting. For the first time, I was passionate about something positive. I was cast in a variety of high school plays and absolutely loving life.

While on-stage, I felt rejuvenated. I felt as though I could perform any role and perform it well. I felt as though people would now have to pay attention to me when I spoke.

At sixteen, I received the "Outstanding Speech Award" and was honored (with a bouquet of long-stemmed red roses) at a ceremony in front of the entire school. The presenter was Carol Gorton, the Dean of Girls who nearly had me expelled.

These new found treasures proved to me that God was real and that He loved me. *My life had purpose!*

College

The prospect of attending college was exciting. My parents gave me the choice to either enroll in a local college while living at home, or reside on campus at Cal State University Northridge ("CSUN"). I craved independence, so the decision was simple.

In order to be accepted to CSUN, I needed a high grade point average and strong SAT scores. I had gotten "A's" in all high school theatre classes (even set design and building), but since I didn't care about any subject other than theater, grades in my other classes (except English) were low. My GPA had to increase, so I asked my very intelligent dad and brother to write some of my papers.

In fact, *my* best report ever, "Psychoanalyzing August Strindberg," was written by my brother. He must have done a great job, because I received an "A" on the report!

After enduring the SAT three times and being tutored by the Sylvan Learning Center, I took the ACT (comparable to the SAT). (During the exam break, my parents took me out for a delicious ice cream soda!) and ...

I found the "Acceptance" letter from CSUN on the kitchen table with a note from my mom saying, "YOU DID IT!" *(I still have that note.)* Actually, I couldn't have done it without the help of my parents and brother.

College was awesome. At seventeen, I moved into the dorms at the Northridge Campus Residence. Theatre Arts was my major and I was involved in acting, directing, and make-up. I went to school during the day, had rehearsals and/or workshops at night, and then worked as a waitress from midnight until eight in the morning. I slept between school and rehearsals. I was constantly busy, but I loved it - I lived and breathed theatre.

At one time, I was involved in six productions, along with school and workshops, and broke out in a horrific rash.

Acting Career and Jobs

After graduating with a Theatre Arts degree, I continued pursuing a career in acting. While performing at the Group Repertory Theatre - a theatre company in Burbank, CA, I met a wonderful man and actor, Alan Koss, who was a recurring actor in the comedy show "Cheers." Alan and I were cast as father and thirteen-year-old daughter *(I looked young back then)* in a play called "The Deepest Hunger" *(not "The Hunger Games")*. We developed a father-daughter relationship which continues to this day - thirty-one years later. He and his wife, June, are like family!

Unfortunately, at this time, my acting career came with little income. In fact, the IRS called it a "hobby." Although I was insulted by the IRS' comments, I believed that I would soon prove them wrong by earning a substantial amount of money doing what I loved.

In the meantime, however, bills needed to be paid, so I landed a variety of jobs including "temporary" positions through the Apple One agency. This type of work allowed me the freedom to attend acting auditions.

Many times, I would work for months in the same position and be requested back again when the spot re-opened. Mostly, I worked at ABC, CBS, NBC, and Paramount Pictures as an assistant to executives within an industry that I so loved.

While working at NBC, I went to the studio's graphics department to have my acting resume photocopied. That was the day that I met NBC's Graphic Designer Garfield Andre Thompson. We became instant friends and, of course, he made copies of my resume - for FREE! Garfield and his sweet wife, Yvette, have remained part of our family for over thirty years.

At one point, I accepted a full-time job with a non-profit organization *(I even had my own office!)*. As "West Coast Coordinator," I organized and planned formal events, designed newsletters, and wrote and submitted grants within the entertainment industry. Although the job was satisfying to my brain *(and ego!)*, the "power" attached to it caused me to make some bad choices. I wound up leaving the job and my friends behind. *To this day, I am still sorrowful about my actions!*

Someone New

During my early twenties, I was in excellent physical condition. Often I would go to a restaurant/club called "China Trader" where I would dance and get an aerobics "work-out" to a band called "Slow Burn." Many times I would get offers to dance, but when I didn't, I had no problem dancing alone - fully clothed, of course!

On January 8, 1983, I went to the China Trader with my best friend, Jennifer Barlow - a blond haired, blue-eyed bombshell *(does the word "bombshell" date me?)*. A good looking guy full of charisma asked Jennifer to dance. I thought to myself, "If she says no, then I'll say yes." This was unusual because my attitude would normally be, "I'm nobody's second choice," so when Jennifer declined his offer and he asked me, I said, "Yes."

Little did I know that from that point on, my life would take on a whole new direction.

I was impressed by the way that my dance partner spun, twisted, and dipped me on the dance floor. After having an incredible time, he asked for my phone number and said that he would call the next day at noon. However, I wanted nothing to do with a new relationship, so I really didn't want to hear from him. My simple life consisted of work, acting, and an occasional free meal while on a date.

The following day, at exactly twelve o'clock, he called and invited me to a private party that evening at the Castaways Restaurant. I wasn't going to consent until he shared that the event would have unlimited sushi and a caricature artist. To my surprise, I had a great time! He was like no one I had ever met - SMART, FUN, CONFIDENT, and FULL OF LIFE! AND, to top it off, he had a high paying position in the car business.

It wasn't long before my love for acting took a back seat to my love for Alfred ("Al").

Moving In

Soon after we met, Al moved in to my duplex in Burbank, CA. I liked having his clothes in my closet because I could usually find money in the pockets (which he told me that I could have). *My part-time job of searching through clothing was fun!*

Life with Al was a continual adventure. His positive outlook on life, even though he carried deep rooted pain with regard to his family, was intriguing. Al's self-confidence and his love for God were comforting to me. When I was with him, my struggles with rejection and feelings of insecurity were greatly diminished.

I had just graduated from college and was working at New England Life Insurance as the Regional Manager's Assistant. Al had a successful career as Fleet and Leasing Manager in the car business ... UNTIL three months into our relationship when I was given the news that Al had quit his job. *Later, I came to find out that when he and I met, he had already thought about leaving the job.* This was disturbing because the last thing I wanted to do was to support my boyfriend.

Al landed various jobs within the car industry, including a sales position at Victory Porsche Audi in North Hollywood. To kick off their new store, management informed employees that the top salesman of the month was going to drive a Porsche for the following thirty days. So, when a beautiful BRAND NEW red PORSCHE showed up outside my door, I was very impressed by the handsome gentleman who was driving.

When he wasn't working and between jobs, Al played a lot of tennis. During high school, he was the number one tennis player, and had circumstances with his family been different, he could have been a pro!

Five and a half years into our relationship, I was ready to get married. I was getting older - twenty-nine - and my "biological clock" was ticking. I wanted very badly to have children, but first needed to be a wife. Al wasn't in agreement with this plan initially, so I asked him to leave so that I could be available for someone else. He packed his bags, said good-bye, and two days later, came back and said, "Okay, let's get married."

Marriage

Al has been a HUGE Los Angeles Dodgers fan since he was young. At eleven years old, instead of doing homework at a classmate's house (like he told his parents), he would take a bus and head straight for the stadium. *The bus ride to and from Dodger Stadium - along with two hot dogs - cost a whopping two dollars!* By the time he was twelve, he had gone to every home game. By thirteen, he worked at the stadium selling programs. Shortly after, he was promoted to "Coca-Cola" salesman and was selling Coca Cola glass bottles to the fans.

Fast forward a dozen years to the year 1988 when we were making wedding plans. After searching for months, I finally found what seemed to be the "perfect" wedding venue. When I told Al that the wedding was to be held less than a mile from Dodger Stadium in Elysian Park and that the date was going to be October 15, he just smiled and said, "It will be opening day of the World Series that day and the Dodgers will be playing!"

He contacted friends whom he knew would be buying tickets to the game and forced them to promise that they would be at our wedding and not at the game. They laughed at Al because the wedding was still over four months away and the Dodgers were currently only in third place.

Al was right. October 15, 1988 was the first night of the World Series between the Dodgers and the Oakland A's … AND it was the night of Kurt Gibson's famous World Series home run … AND it was the night of our wedding. Since our celebration was practically next door to Dodger Stadium, the Good Year Blimp hovered over our wedding (and over the baseball game). We could hear loud cheering coming from the stadium while Al and I were sharing our "I do's." It seemed as though we had invited 56,000 of our closest friends to the wedding!

It was a great wedding - planned by me. *I was gifted in multi-tasking in those days!* I felt a little guilty for our "Dodger Fan" guests who missed the historic Dodgers game, but at least they were able to partake of free dancing, food, and an open bar! Our friend, Steve, gave us one of our favorite wedding presents - matching World Series Dodgers T-shirts.

The Honeymoon

It was awful! World Series games on the television EVERY NIGHT - and I don't even like baseball! What made it worse is that the town of Morro Bay goes to sleep at ten o'clock - the time that most of the Dodgers' games ended.

We did get to go for a boat ride (on the only day that it didn't rain) EXCEPT when the boat stopped moving due to a leak. We were stuck IN THE MIDDLE OF THE BAY bailing water from our sinking boat. And, I had to go to the bathroom IN THE MIDDLE OF THE BAY. *I vowed that my husband would make this up to me someday!*

Okay, the good part of the honeymoon was that the hotel room - known as the "mini suite" had a large jacuzzi tub. So, while my husband was talking (loudly) to "his" Dodgers through the TV, I was attempting to relax amidst the soothing bubbles.

A New Little Addition

It had been my dream from a very young age to have a daughter. So, in 1990, when Lana (named after my Nana Lylla) was born, I was ecstatic. Her fingers and toes were so small; I kept looking to make sure that they were all there. She was a seven pound half-an-ounce beautiful and perfect gift.

Lana was born with a severe case of jaundice, probably because she was two weeks late (and still had to be induced in order to come out). Daddy Al held her under the lights, and although the nurse offered to lay her in a crib, Al insisted on holding his little girl. The doctor told us that we could either leave her at the hospital or take her home with special "jaundice" equipment. There was no discussion - we brought her home.

This was a challenging time. As first time parents, we barely knew how to change a diaper, let alone provide medical care for our newborn. Nurses came daily to help with breastfeeding *(which was another struggle)* and to check on Lana. After a difficult and exhausting week, the jaundice subsided.

For the next eleven months, Lana rarely cried; she seemed to be a healthy and content baby. We never opened a baby food jar - her food was home-made by her daddy and included a mixture of mommy's milk, fruit, and baby cereal.

We were with her every moment and she was our whole world!

My mom and dad were the best grandparents ever. My dad used to say, "My job is to shop for diapers." It was heart-warming for me to witness the relationship between my daughter and my parents.

Al's dad, Grandpa Alfred Sr., and his wife, Grandma Adriana, also loved and cared deeply for Lana. Alfred Sr. used to call Lana "Bubaloopsky." *Actually, he referred to his skunk, cat, and those he loved as "Bubaloopsky" too!*

Al's mom, Jackie, and her husband, Alexander, were crazy about their new granddaughter, Lana, as well.

Our bundle of joy!

Devastation

Prior to Lana's first birthday, our lives took a drastic turn. Lana had been lethargic and wasn't eating much, so we took her to a pediatrician who told us that she had lost weight and needed to eat. He prescribed antibiotics and released her. At home, we noticed that swelling had developed under her eyes, so we contacted her pediatrician again. He told us that there was nothing he could do and that we needed to call an eye doctor. After asking certain questions, the eye doctor told us that she needed to be seen by a pediatrician. Nobody knew anything.

Soon after, Grandma Adriana urged us to take Lana to Children's Hospital in Los Angeles.

In the hospital's waiting room, Lana died in my arms of heart failure. She was rushed to the intensive care unit where doctors performed CPR.

Al and I insisted on being in her room, even though the staff tried to stop us.

"While our daughter is fighting for her life, we will be right here with her," we said. Al was praying to the Lord while I was in the back of her hospital room. I was saying to Lana: "Take a breath - you can do it!"

Doctors and nurses were repeating things like, "We're losing her" and "100, 90, 60, 40, 15" (speaking of her heart rate) and then, "Okay, she's back." This went on throughout the night.

Al insisted on finding out what Lana's chances were, so after Lana was FINALLY stable, the nurse told Al that Lana had a FIFTY PERCENT CHANCE OF SURVIVING THE WEEKEND."

It felt as though my heart dropped to the ground - I could hardly breathe!

Lana's diagnosis went from "Congestive Heart Failure" to "End Stage Cardiac Disease" and "Idiopathic Dilated Cardiomyopathy." Lana was hooked up to a respirator and numerous other machines and equipment.

She weighed only eleven pounds (Al called it her "fighting weight") and was so tiny.

Another Child - Not Now!

I was in such shock and desperation that even though I didn't smoke, I took a few hits of my husband's cigarette. In the middle of the third puff, something came over me: *"What if I'm pregnant?"*

The next day, I found out that I was indeed pregnant. A troubling question kept running through my mind: *"Could God be replacing Lana with a new baby?"*

Even though we had been trying to have another baby, I wouldn't have chosen for this wonderful blessing to come in the middle of this horrendous storm.

Searching for Something Good

Lana's nurse instructed me to go home and pump breast milk.

"Good," I thought, *"something that I can do to help my daughter."*

When I returned to the hospital with a full bottle of breast milk, I was told that my milk would no longer be useful.

After breast feeding Lana for nearly a year, I was heartbroken to learn that I would no longer be able to provide nourishment for my daughter.

Lana Turns One

On August 24, 1991 (eight days after being admitted to the hospital), Lana turned a year old. I couldn't believe that my baby and I would be spending her first birthday in the hospital.

This was such a depressing and sad time!

My mom had offered to buy a "birthday" cake, but since Lana wasn't able to celebrate, my parents purchased a cake which had on it the words, "Thank you, Lana's doctors and nurses."

It was our way to show appreciation for all of the doctors, nurses, and staff who cared so much about Lana.

Holding My Baby

All I wanted to do was to hold my baby, but she was so surrounded by equipment, tubes, and wires that to hold Lana could put her in danger. However, in spite of the risks (and cautious nurses), Dr. Arno Hohn, Lana's wonderful doctor and Head Cardiologist at Children's Hospital, allowed me to hold Lana for a few minutes each day. He asked Lana's nurses, "What would you want to do if this were your daughter?"

Holding Lana was my favorite part of the day. Some of the time, though, her tubing would get tangled and I would have to give her back to the nurses. Those precious moments with my daughter would be cut short.

These were agonizing times!

Since we were not allowed to stay in Lana's ICU room during the night, my parents paid for Al and me to stay at a nearby hotel. We used the hotel only for sleeping. The rest of the time, we lived in Lana's hospital room. Each morning before returning to the hospital, we would call to find out how Lana was doing. These phone calls were horrible because we were often told that she had barely survived the night.

One morning when we arrived at the hospital, we found doctors and nurses around Lana's bed performing CPR. What we didn't know was that during the night, Lana had been moved to a different room and that the patient who was receiving CPR wasn't Lana. They neglected to let us know of this change before we showed up. Al fell to the ground because of fear and relief.

We were on "pins and needles" and could barely keep it together! AND, I was pregnant!

Heart Transplant - Her Only Chance

After being in the ICU for weeks, Dr. Hohn informed us that Children's Hospital could do nothing more for Lana and that Loma Linda University Medical Center would be her only hope. He told us that, even with Loma Linda's advanced equipment, Lana wouldn't be able to breathe on her own and that a heart transplant would be her only chance.

This was deeply distressing. Since the first heart transplant had been performed only five years earlier on "Baby Moses" (by Dr. Leonard Bailey at Loma Linda University's Heart Center), this was a relatively new field.

My parents encouraged us to contact the families of transplant recipients. We found that some of the challenges included:
Heart rejection, a fragile immune system, frequent doctor visits and tests, blood work, and a variety of side effects from the heart medication.

Despite the challenges, we learned that transplanted children were living somewhat "normal" lives.

Although it was an extremely difficult decision, we decided to place Lana on the heart transplant list.

This was a scary and emotional time, especially when we knew we would have to leave the doctors and staff at Children's Hospital who were such a blessing to us.

Loma Linda University Medical Center

While making arrangements for Lana and a medical team to be transported by helicopter to Loma Linda, we were informed that a heart was available for her. We signed the documents, and as the helicopter showed up to take our daughter away, Al and I drove to the hospital. Lana was admitted to the Intensive Care Unit and hooked up to a respirator and various other equipment.

When we got there, we were told that the heart wasn't a match for Lana. This news was somewhat of a relief for us, as we weren't quite ready to embark upon this course of action.

Hours later, Lana's oxygen levels improved and she no longer needed a respirator. This had to be a miracle, since Dr. Hohn from Children's Hospital had told us that it would be impossible for her to breathe on her own. The respirator was removed.

Was there a chance that she wouldn't need a heart transplant after all?

A decision had to be made - should Lana remain on the heart transplant list, or should she be released to go home?

Two doctors felt that Lana wouldn't survive without the surgery. Another of her doctors thought that she might be okay without it. "Dr. Dad" (Al) believed that she would do well at home.

Al had become much like a doctor through this experience with his daughter; he had God-guided intuition about Lana's medical needs. He understood how each machine and medication worked; he even knew which procedures could cause her permanent damage.

One particular time when Lana's heart was beating erratically, doctors looked up her condition in the medical books (no "Google" back then) to find the proper dosage of medication. Dr. Dad insisted that the books' recommended amounts be decreased by ninety percent. The doctors followed Al's advice, and even at ten percent of the suggested dosage, the medicine was too strong for Lana's weakened body. Had the doctors followed the medical guidelines and not listened to Dr. Dad, Lana would surely have died.

Time to Go Home

Against the recommendation of two of her doctors, Lana was home! It was as though we had a new-born baby, as she had to learn to walk and talk all over again. In spite of obvious challenges and concerns, like the continual monitoring of Lana's health, along with keeping ourselves, visitors, and the apartment germ-free, we were thrilled to be home!

It was difficult to discern her condition, as she was a joyful baby who rarely cried or complained. Even in the midst of her hospitalizations, Lana was emotionally strong and content with whatever was going on at the time. My dad used to refer to her as a "soldier!"

Here We Go Again

During their visit a couple of months later, my parents expressed concern that Lana did not seem well.

We took her back to Children's Hospital where she was found to be in respiratory distress. On January 2, 1992, Lana was admitted to the ICU. After being hooked up to a respirator, it was discovered that both lungs had collapsed AND she had "RSV," a deadly respiratory infection which had taken the lives of many children throughout the hospital.

Lana was a little over a year old and was fighting for her life - AGAIN. Al and I were having a heated argument which was so disruptive that he was asked to leave the hospital. *This was VERY stressful!*

A few minutes later, there was an intense look of helplessness on Lana's face which I will never forget. Her heart stopped beating and she went into full cardiac arrest. The doctors and nurses rushed into her room to perform CPR. This went on a few times throughout the night.

Just like months before (when we had first taken Lana to the hospital and she had died in my arms of heart failure), doctors were repeating the words, "We're losing her," as they counted her heart rate down from "100" to "10."

Again, when the nurses asked me to leave, I insisted on remaining in her room. I stayed behind the curtain and told the nurse, "You have your job and I have mine." The nurse left me alone while I prayed to God that if He saved Lana, we would agree to putting her back on the list for a heart transplant.

Though barely hanging on, Lana was still alive. Al returned to the room shortly after our fight (he had never left the hospital) and we became a united team for the well-being of our daughter.

Neurologist's Report

In addition to collapsed lungs, a deadly virus, and recent episodes of cardiac arrest, the neurologist's report was the worst news of all: "Lana is brain dead."

WE WERE DEVASTATED!

I asked the neurologists if there was the slightest possibility that she was just too exhausted to wake up. Their faces told it all - the diagnosis of "brain dead" remained.

I was an emotional wreck. We called Al's mom, Jackie, who firmly advised us to stay in the hospital room with Lana at all times and to not leave her side. This was perfect advice and from that point on, we decided that one of us would always be with our daughter.

Even though Lana seemed incoherent, I chose to believe that she could hear every word. I reminded her that she was going to have a brother or sister in the next few months and that, although dying would be understandable, being "brain dead" would not be an option.

As I was talking, Lana's arm and leg moved up and down abruptly. When I asked about Lana's movements, our favorite nurse, Nida, said that these were common indications of brain dead activity. As I couldn't allow myself to focus on anything negative, I went back to talking with Lana.

Suddenly, Lana opened her eyes and looked at me, then the nurse, and back at me again. I asked Nida, "What was that?" She replied, "I'll be right back." Nida ran down the hall and brought in the doctor. As Dr. Hohn shined the light into Lana's eyes, he noticed that one of her pupils was slightly dilated.

We were ecstatic, as was the hospital ward, for the first time in a very long time.

There was a sliver of hope for my baby!

Could This Have Been a Miracle?

I will always remember the two neurologists holding their clipboards as they reported: "We must have made a mistake; she's neurologically normal." Those words still send chills down my spine.

This had to be a miracle from God!

Complications

Although neurologically normal, Lana's heart was rapidly deteriorating and her heart rate had increased to well over two hundred. Each beat was damaging her heart and the heart muscle was being replaced by scar tissue.

In order to keep Lana alive, she was placed on a drug called Norcuron, which rendered her temporarily paralyzed and unable to communicate.

THESE WERE TERRIFYING TIMES! I felt so helpless!

Al had asked the Head Cardiologist at Children's Hospital to treat Lana as though she was his granddaughter, so when Dr. Hohn told my husband, "Lana's gotta get back to Loma Linda because she will die if she stays here," we listened to the doctor.

The next day, our wonderful Dr. Hohn came to say "good-bye" in his "grandpa's" suit and tie. It was difficult to again leave the doctors, nurses, and staff, who had become like family.

Dr. Hohn wanted Lana to have the best care, so he arranged for his head nurse to accompany Lana in the ambulance. The nurse was instructed to stay at Loma Linda until Lana was completely situated.

Heart Transplant Not Possible

We now knew that Lana's only hope would be to have a new heart. However, she could not be placed on the list because both of her lungs were infected and if her body were to be opened up, the infection would spread and she would likely die. We prayed for a miracle. We just wanted our little girl back.

At this time, I was six months pregnant. I needed to take care of myself because of the baby inside of me, but it wasn't easy. With each bite of food, I fought feelings of guilt because I knew that my daughter was unable to eat. My parents came from Vegas often and took Al and me out for meals so that we could stay healthy.

Life was HARD and I was tired - really tired!

Encouragement

One day, the hospital chaplain gave me a
paper which had a verse from the Bible. To
date, it is my favorite:

⁴"Fear not, for I am with you;
Be not dismayed, for I am your God.
I will strengthen you,
Yes, I will help you,
I will uphold you with My righteous right hand."

It gave me comfort to know that God was
with me in the "heart of the storm." To
be uplifted every time we entered Lana's
room, the above verse, along with family
pictures, were placed on the wall of her
hospital room. Whenever we transferred
rooms, this scripture and the photos
moved with us.

Hope

Despite the horrendous medical reports and circumstances, Al remained positive and hopeful and wanted to portray only peaceful emotions to Lana.

One day, a good friend of ours came to the hospital. As Marie walked down the hallway, it was obvious that she was in a highly emotional state, so we kept her from seeing Lana. It was not easy for us to send her away, but necessary.

Al was firm about not showing sadness or remorse to our daughter, which I believe was instrumental to Lana's strength and courage.

Money Isn't Everything

In 1991, many companies were required by law to have a ride-share program with an incentive package for participating employees. We designed and wrote these plans and submitted them to the South Coast Air Quality Management District.

We hired a wonderful young lady who helped us by setting appointments and assisting with Lana. It was the perfect business for Al and me, as we could work together while raising our child.

Since my husband is an excellent salesman and businessman, we had many clients. As we were becoming financially "set," we learned that in order for Lana to receive a heart transplant, we would have to live within twenty miles of Loma Linda. At the time, our home was over sixty miles away.

This was serious. Al had appointments every day and if we moved, he would have to travel long distances. We were both essential to Lana's care, so Al needed to be available.

The decision was simple - the business had to go. Our daughter was infinitely more important to us than money!

Friends and family tried to convince us to keep the business since Lana was going to die anyway. We would hear none of that and began looking for an apartment close to Loma Linda.

Heart Transplant - Is This the Time?

The heart transplant team was scheduled to meet three days from that time to decide whether or not Lana would be healthy enough to be placed on the heart transplant list. Her lungs were getting better, but at this point, the infection was still there.

Two days later, before the transplant team had the chance to reconvene, we received a call from Joyce Johnston, our favorite heart transplant coordinator, who told us that a heart was available. "Dr. Dad" got on the phone, and asked, "Are you sure that her infection is gone?" Joyce didn't know, so Al asked to speak to the surgeon. When Joyce told Al that the surgeon wouldn't be able to contact him, Al said, "Well, then no heart transplant."

Shortly after, a call came in from the surgeon, Dr. Razzouk. When Al asked about Lana's chances on the operating table, the doctor replied that the normal survival rate for a heart transplant would be eighty percent, but due to Lana's possible infection, her odds would only be fifty percent. Al said to the doctor: "Lana has been through too much to have this surgery with such low odds." Dr. Razzouk asked, "So, you're turning down the heart?" to which Al responded: "Yes."

A few minutes later, we received a call from Dr. Chinnock, Lana's heart doctor, who asked Al, "Are you crazy - do you know how many children die while waiting for a heart?" Al explained his views, and needless to say, Lana's doctor was not happy.

Some hours later, Dr. Chinnock called again saying, "Somebody up there must really love you - another heart has come in. Lana was tested and the infection is gone. A whole new surgical team is ready to go."

On Monday, January 27, 1992, Lana was about to receive a heart transplant. It would be the two hundred and second heart transplant to ever have been attempted on children.

We were excited, scared, and faithful at the same time. As Lana was being wheeled in for surgery, we placed a miniature Bible inside her diaper.

The Long Wait

During Lana's six hour surgery, Al and I sat in the lobby (under the picture on the wall of Jesus and little children), until - FINALLY, the elevator doors opened and out came the surgeon.

Surgery - Complete!

The doctor reported the news that the surgery went as well as could be expected. *Our seventeen-month-old little girl received a new heart!*

From that point on, we referred to Dr. Gundry as "Dr. God" because of his beautiful countenance, white beard, and his God-given giftings.

We will be forever grateful for the family who chose to give their child's heart so that our daughter could live!

My parents arrived at the hospital (from Vegas) and found me asleep on the floor of the waiting room. (I was seven months pregnant at the time.) Although we weren't allowed in Lana's room, we could watch from outside her window. We noticed that the miniature Bible had been moved from inside her diaper to above her body.

While Lana was still asleep, my parents took Al and me to breakfast. *I still remember the tasty pancakes!*

The next forty-eight hours were critical, as this is often the time when the new heart goes into rejection. The ICU team, clothed in hospital garb, kept a close eye on Lana.

Moving Day - Bittersweet!

On February 1, 1992, we packed up our belongings and moved from Glendale to an apartment in Upland, CA (The Oaks). At the same time, Lana's breathing tube was being removed. Although Al and I were excited to live closer to the hospital, the move to Upland took an entire day and we couldn't be with Lana during her procedure.

When we finally got to the hospital, Lana could talk and there was no longer a tube down her throat. She was also taken off the "paralyzing drug" Norcuron.

I almost forgot how pretty her mouth was and how much I loved to hear her speak! It was a joyful moment!

Finally Home

I'll never forget that special Valentine's Day in 1992 when we took Lana home from the hospital. I rocked her on my very pregnant belly for hours. After, we laid her in bed between us as she repeatedly turned her head back and forth to look at Al and me until she fell asleep.

I was grateful that the Lord answered our prayers and gave us our little girl back. It was the best Valentine's Day ever!

Lana was highly susceptible to infection, due to immunity weakening effects of the anti-rejection medications (which she took seventeen times a day). We needed to be clean and germ-free, because illness or infection could lead to her death.

Despite all that she had been through, this was the first time in a long time that Lana was happy and laughing regularly. *She was glad to be home … and we were glad to have her home with us!*

Another Little Blessing

On the morning of April 17, 1992, Lana had a doctor's appointment at Loma Linda. That same afternoon, I was scheduled to give birth to Lana's brother at Glendale Adventist Medical Center (many miles away).

I'll never forget asking another family if we could go in front of them to see the doctor, as we needed to get to Glendale in a HURRY.

We made it - and that evening at eight minutes past ten, Alfred Loera, III ("Alfie") was born.

I will always remember the first time that Lana looked at her brother and the love that she had for him.

Caring for a new-born and a frail eighteen-month-old was quite the challenge. Everyone and everything had to be clean and healthy. Both children were so vulnerable.

I walked around with a diaper in one hand and a baby in the other. My family used to tell me that "the baby(ies) don't need to be changed right now." I would say, "Well, they will soon!" *I was ready.*

Their sleep schedule was less than ideal. Lana didn't fall asleep until late at night and Alfie woke up with the roosters (early, early!).

These were tiresome times, but my husband and I were oh so grateful!

Brother and Sister Relationship - How Sweet it is!

As babies, Lana and Alfie laughed and talked with each other in a language that no one else understood. They had a special bond and loved being together. Every day, we placed them on their swings and they rocked back and forth while watching "Sesame Street."

Lana was very protective of her baby brother. When Alfie was eight months old, he fell asleep standing up while leaning on a chair (with his pillow). We wanted to put him to bed, but Lana blocked us so that we couldn't wake him.

Baby Alfie was intelligent, independent, strong, and fearless. This was a challenging combination for which precautions had to be made. The apartment was baby-proofed and safe. His bedroom (shared with his sister) consisted of a mattress on the floor, along with many toys and books (which he would sometimes destroy). He was a happy and content baby.

At age one, in a diaper and t-shirt, Alfie opened our front door, walked down the stairs, and took off running across the lawn to the apartment manager's office. When Alfie arrived at the office, he opened the door and attempted to help himself to the candy on the front desk, but was too little to reach the "goods."

We used to say that if we left him alone, he would be the youngest person to ever run away from home.

When they were little, I would take Lana and Alfie for daily walks in their double stroller. Sometimes, our dear friend, Valerie, and her daughter, Jamyce, would join us. *We referred to Valerie as the "boogedy-boogedy woman" which was taken from a Sesame Street episode.* Valerie loved to dress Alfie (red and blue were her favorites), but I was comfortable keeping him in a diaper and t-shirt - it was easier to change diapers that way!

Alfie grew to be a "relatively" low maintenance child *(did I say "relatively?")*, except for the fact that he had an unlimited amount of energy and the impulse to go after whatever he desired at any given moment. Also, he was fearless. His sister was like a "mommy" to him, so she would let us know if there were any concerns.

One time when we were visiting my parents, my dad asked Lana where her brother was. She replied, "He's up there." Alfie had moved a chair next to the table, climbed on the table, and was swinging from the chandelier.

Throughout their childhood, Lana and Alfie were the best of friends. Whenever Lana didn't feel well, she would ask for her brother who would always find a way to cheer her up or to make her laugh.

Alfie is crazy about his sister!

Spinal Meningitis

When Lana was two and a half, she had a temperature of over one hundred and four degrees. We tried waking her, but she wouldn't budge; we tried talking to her, but she wouldn't respond.

She was incoherent and I was FILLED WITH FEAR!

We immediately left for the hospital. When we arrived at eleven o'clock at night, we were greeted by Dr. Chinnock, a wonderful man of God who had been Lana's heart doctor since she was eleven months old. Dr. Chinnock happened to be in the emergency room checking on a patient.

He didn't know that on that night, he would have another patient - his Lana!

Dr. Chinnock believed that Lana had Spinal Meningitis and told us that if medication wasn't started right away, she probably wouldn't survive.

I had never heard of Spinal Meningitis and didn't know how serious it could be.

When I called to let my parents know what was happening, my mom shared her fears and said that she and my dad were on their way.

Lana was admitted to the ICU and medication for Spinal Meningitis was started within minutes. *We believe that any other doctor would have ordered a series of tests prior to diagnosis, and Lana would have died during the wait.*

Dr. Chinnock said that he could picture the Lord turning toward Lana and blessing her. He prayed the following over Lana:

> [5]*"The Lord bless you and keep you;*
> *The Lord make His face shine upon you,*
> *And be gracious to you;*
> *The Lord look upon you with favor,*
> *And give you peace."*

We placed the above verse on the wall in Lana's hospital room.

By the time my parents arrived, a miracle had happened and within the course of a few hours, Lana had gone from being incoherent to being slightly coherent.

My parents took Alfie back to Vegas with them. For the next few weeks, all of our time was spent by Lana's side (except for the two hours when the nurses changed shifts).

After three LONG weeks of testing, poking, medicating, prodding and icing (to reduce fevers), Lana was released to go home. My parents brought Alfie back to us, too.

Our family was together again!

1996 - A Bad Year

The pressures of life and our daughter's illnesses took a toll on our marriage and my husband turned to alcohol as never before. Things had become so unbearable that in 1996, the kids and I moved into my parents' home in Las Vegas. I hated asking my family for help, but I had nowhere else to turn.

These were awful times!

Life in Las Vegas

After a few weeks, I enrolled the kids in school - Lana in first grade and Alfie in kindergarten - and we rented an apartment. We saw my parents nearly every day and they were fully involved in our lives. They helped the kids with their school work and even had a relationship with their teachers.

In Alfie's kindergarten class, the teacher had asked the families to collect aluminum cans in order to raise money for supplies. My parents wanted to help, so they carried around hefty bags as they "cleaned up the neighborhood."

One time, the teacher heard a sound coming from one of the bags my parents had given her. When she opened the bag, to her surprise, out leaped a lizard! The class was making so much money that the teacher kindly asked that my parents stop collecting cans.

Although Mom and Dad were wonderful and I treasured our times together, I felt alone in my quiet apartment. I missed Al and kept reminding myself of the reasons I left, because it was never my plan for us to separate.

In spite of everything, I loved my husband.

Al was still living in our Upland apartment and we talked often. He was seeking the Lord's help with the hope that he would someday be with his family again.

I had made a commitment to the apartment leasing company and to my parents that we would remain in Las Vegas for a minimum of six months. However, something horrible happened which shortened our stay.

Alfie developed a minor case of Chicken Pox and I developed a major sore throat. I paid little attention to my health (I had not been able to eat solid food for days and could barely swallow) and focused more on the possibility that Lana could contract Chicken Pox along with her brother.

As I watched, I noticed red spots on her body and drainage coming from her ear. The doctor said that these were not signs of Chicken Pox and that she needed to be hospitalized as soon as possible.

It was a miserable drive from Las Vegas to Upland. We had to continually stop the car because of Lana's vomiting (which also wasn't a sign of Chicken Pox). I was in excruciating physical pain, due to my throat, and excruciating emotional pain, due to the suffering of my daughter.

In addition, the situation was awkward since we hadn't seen my husband in weeks AND we were going back to stay with him in our old apartment.

Red Spots - A Mystery

The next morning, Al drove Lana to the hospital and she was immediately admitted into the intensive care unit.

While I was at home, I received a call from one of the nurses: "What was the color of Lana's skin this morning when you last saw her?" I told the nurse that Lana had a few red spots that I thought were probably Chicken Pox." "Well," said the nurse, "Her whole body is now covered in red spots."

"WHAT?!? Are you sure you have the right child?" I wanted to believe that they had made a mistake, but no mistake had been made.

In order to reduce high fevers, Lana was being iced regularly and placed on strong medicine.

I felt so helpless, as I couldn't be with my beautiful six-year-old daughter due to my illness.

Again, my parents came and took Alfie back to Vegas with them.

Many tests were done to discover what was wrong with Lana. An infectious disease doctor was called in and still tests were inconclusive. The diagnosis was narrowed down to Scarlet Fever, Measles, Kawasaki's Disease or a severe viral infection.

It was eventually concluded that Lana probably had Scarlet Fever. At the same time, I was diagnosed with Strep Throat, which is highly contagious and can lead to Scarlet Fever.

I was terrified to learn that my illness could have caused my daughter's death.

Since I was sick, I wasn't able to see Lana for nearly a week. This was the longest period of time that I was ever away from her. *It was so hard!*

Lana spent weeks in the intensive care unit. FINALLY, the spots and fever disappeared and and she was free to go home.

Moving Back to Upland

I couldn't go back to living in Las Vegas anymore. I was home with my husband in California and close to the hospital.

Although my parents were able to get us out of the Vegas apartment lease, they now had to adjust to the fact that we weren't going to be living close to them anymore. I felt horrible and wished that I could be two places at one time. I thoroughly enjoyed having my mom and dad by my side and don't know what I would have done without them!

I began a journey of juggling my marriage, home-schooling, medical care, social events, and hospital visits. Even with our best efforts to keep her from germs, Lana battled with ear infections, colds, fevers, and severe headaches. Yet, she rarely complained about her health or lack of a "normal" social life.

She was, after all, a soldier!

My Friend Janice

During our eight year stay at the Upland apartment, something (or someone) happened that changed my life forever. Janice, her husband and two children, moved into the complex and we became friends. We often had coffee together as we talked about the challenges in our lives.

Although Janice had been going through major disappointments and difficulties, she had an amazing peace about her that I had never witnessed. I wanted to know more, so I asked, "What's different about you - I have to know." She answered simply, "It's Jesus."

Janice shared that when she accepted Jesus Christ into her life, she experienced an inner peace that the world had never provided for her.

Growing up, I felt as though something was missing - that there must have been more to life than what I was able to see with my eyes. I now found myself wondering if this

"Jesus" could have been the missing link. *Could He bring me the same kind of inner peace that I witnessed in Janice?*

I began pondering the subject of "faith," and recognized that faith is the belief that something is real even though we can't see it. Just as we experience the effects of wind, gravity, and air, but don't actually see these things, it seemed as though this is where "faith" would come in. I realized, too, that anything to do with God would require faith.

Since I believed with all my heart that God existed, I asked myself, *"Could it also be true that Jesus was real and that He was connected to God?"*

I had an intense desire to know the truth, so even though it felt awkward, I prayed: *"Jesus, if you're real, show me."*

Heart Rejection - Seeking Help

Doctors had informed us from the beginning of this "heart transplant" journey that even with medication, heart rejection often occurs and is often fatal. What makes it especially difficult is that many times there are no signs that the body is "rejecting."

Since the transplanted heart wasn't the heart that Lana was born with, other organs attempt to attack this "new" heart. In order to disguise the new organ, medication must be taken each day. Unfortunately, side effects of the medicine cause Lana to have a low immune system and a vulnerability to infection and disease.

Throughout the years, Lana had several bouts of heart rejection. Each time, she was in the ICU, and each time, we almost lost her.

The time coming up, however, would most definitely be the worst. When Lana was seven years old, we took her in for a routine doctor's visit. She seemed to be in a good mood and I was grateful just to be "visiting" the hospital, instead of "living" in the hospital! Her usual echocardiogram, EKG, and blood tests were performed.

The report came in: "Lana is in the MOST SEVERE STAGE OF HEART REJECTION." She was immediately admitted into the ICU and hooked up to numerous machines.

I was in a state of shock and was even furious at the nurse: "You don't know what you're talking about!" was what I blurted out to her.

My heart was racing and my emotions were all over the map. What if Lana didn't make it? Is this life all there is? Is there really a heaven?

There was nothing more that we could do but to watch our little girl fight for her life - AGAIN! As was her nature, Lana kept smiling as she showed the nurses how to work the hospital equipment.

Al brought Alfie and we checked into a hotel. I opened the drawer by the night stand and found a Bible. In desperation to find an ounce of hope, I opened the book and the following words jumped out at me:

> [6]*"For God so loved the world*
> *that He gave His only begotten Son*
> *that whoever believes in Him*
> *will have everlasting life."*

I had seen these words before (from John 3:16), but never really considered their meaning. As I re-read the sentence and again asked God to reveal Himself to me, I was led to other verses from the Bible:

> [7]*"I am the resurrection and the life.*
> *He who believes in Me,*
> *though he may die, he shall live.*
> *And whoever lives and believes in Me*
> *shall never die."*

At that moment, I experienced a supernatural revelation that is hard to put to words. *I felt closer to God than ever before and knew that Jesus was a part of it.*

Powerful Medication with Powerful Side Effects

When we returned to the ICU the next morning, Lana was hooked up to multiple machines and on massive doses of intravenous medication. The side effects were so powerful that, for the first time in her life, Lana's blood sugar levels skyrocketed. As a result, her finger had to be pricked every hour and when levels were high, she would need insulin shots. Since needles were painful for Lana, this was especially difficult for her and for us.

Except for an occasional break, either Al or I were with Lana, while the other was at home (or at the [8]Ronald McDonald House) with Alfie. Loma Linda graciously provided us with a recliner chair, so that we could spend nights in Lana's room.

With all the bells, whistles, and constant noise permeating the hospital walls, sleep was not easy and I often prayed for morning to arrive.

Whenever Al and I changed shifts, we brought Alfie to the hospital. While Lana was in the ICU, since Alfie was too young to be in her room, we would wheel her into the lobby so that they could be together. While she was in a regular hospital room, Al would cook dinner and bring it so that Lana and Alfie could eat in her room. Alfie was the highlight of Lana's hospital days!

FINALLY, after spending three weeks in the hospital, Lana's heart and blood sugar levels stabilized and she was released to go home. *YEAH!*

While contemplating the recent hospital events, I remembered having heard about "divine intervention." I wondered if what we had just experienced could have been just that - and - here's why:

When the diagnosis came that Lana was in the worst stage of heart rejection, Lana was already at the doctor's office. Since she had not shown any symptoms of the severity of her condition, had we not already been at the hospital, we would probably have lost her. Although God didn't cause this to happen, He was with us throughout the ordeal and blessed Lana with the best possible care at the perfect time and place. I believe that this truly was God's "divine intervention."

Gorman Learning Center

Up to this point, I home-schooled my kids through the school district. This wasn't a good match for us because the district required that we work at the children's actual grade verses their grade level. Lana needed a special education plan and Alfie was advanced beyond his years. I spent nearly a year searching for a program which would be more adaptable to our needs.

Gorman Learning Center, a charter home-school program, allowed me to educate my children at home and be available to leave in the event of an emergency. I was able to teach at the kids' level and classes were available outside the home, along with special education programs and tutors for Lana. And, books and supplies were free!

Cheryl

I met a sweet lady named Cheryl while our kids were in a gymnastics class. Cheryl had a peace about her which reminded me of my friend, Janice. I shared that I had recently registered my kids in Gorman Learning Center and had been waiting (for months) to be assigned a facilitator (one who is credentialed and acts as liaison between the parent and government). I was surprised when Cheryl told me that she currently worked as a facilitator for Gorman. Jumping up, I said, "I want YOU to be my facilitator." Jumping up, she responded, "It has to be me!"

The very next day, someone from Gorman finally called to let me know who my kids' facilitator would be. I told them: "You're too late. We've chosen our facilitator and her name is Cheryl Proulx. Please change your paperwork."

Cheryl soon became my friend and my mentor. She shared that she was a

Christian and that her relationship with Jesus Christ brought meaning to her life that had never been there before. She shared that He is a living God who loves us unconditionally. She explained that the Holy Bible is God's message to us and encouraged me to read it.

Denice - Our New Blessing

Since changes were being made at Gorman, we were sad to learn that Cheryl would no longer be our facilitator. Cheryl prayed that the Lord would provide us with a new person who would deeply care for us. Denice Burchett became my kids' facilitator and my friend. *Today, she is one of my closest friends.*

One day, Denice informed me that our new school books and supplies were ready to be picked up *(always a fun time for me and the kids - like unwrapping Christmas gifts!).* She said that she had been helping at her church's Food Pantry, and that I could meet her there to pick up the "home school goods."

I was excited because I had always wanted to volunteer at a Food Pantry and asked if I could help. She replied, "Sure."

Food Pantry - A Delicious Discovery!

When I first volunteered at Rancho Christian Center's Food Pantry, I met a kind young woman named Roxanne Wilson (who I found out was my friend, Denice's sister). Roxanne asked if I wanted prayer for anything. I was stunned because that question had never been posed to me before. *How could I refuse such a generous offer?*

After I shared some of Lana's medical history and our family's on-going challenges, the Food Pantry team (Roxanne, Denice, Pattie, Sandy, and others) held hands and prayed for us. I had never experienced such love - we were complete strangers, and yet, these caring individuals were pouring out their hearts to God for us. *I was deeply touched.*

When time and health permitted, Lana and I volunteered at the Food Pantry. *Today, eighteen years later, I am honored to direct Rancho Christian Center's Food Pantry.*

Am I Pregnant or Not?

Later, in the year 1999, Lana and I went to a yard sale. At the sale, we met a lovely lady who asked if I could use some maternity clothes, as she had been trying to find a good home for the clothes all day. I politely informed her that I wasn't pregnant. *I don't know if I felt worse for me or for this lady who had just put her foot in her mouth.* (Years later, I found out that after we met, she had said to herself, "Well, at least I won't ever see that poor lady 'me' again.")

Days later, my seven-year-old son, Alfie, was taking the required "STAR" test. Seated next to him was a boy named Travis. As I looked around at the home-schooled families, I noticed a lady who looked familiar and thought to myself, *"Isn't she the one from the yard sale who thought I was pregnant?"* We introduced ourselves and I learned that her name was Ellen Miller and that Alfie's new friend, Travis, was her son!

The next time Lana and I helped at the church's Food Pantry, Ellen was there again. It turned out that Rancho Christian Center was her home church and that she often volunteered at their Food Pantry.

When Ellen and Lana met, there was an immediate connection; Ellen was deeply drawn to Lana, and Lana to Ellen. At the same time, our sons, Alfie and Travis, were developing a close friendship.

Shortly after, Ellen and I became friends. *(Incidentally, I have forgiven her for calling me "pregnant," but we still - eighteen years later - have a big laugh when we remember that time.)* Today, we are the best of friends; she is Lana and Alfie's godmother and I am the godmother to her son, Travis.

A New Relationship

I was now reading the Bible every day and was amazed at how much I felt the Lord's presence while spending time with Him. I was even more amazed to read that He heard all of my prayers and desired a relationship with me:

> *⁹"Draw near to God*
> *and He will draw near to you."*

Also, while reading, the following words seemed to jump out from the page:

> *¹⁰"...then you will call upon Me*
> *and go and pray to Me,*
> *and I will listen to you.*
> *And you will seek Me and find Me,*
> *when you search for Me with all your heart."*

One day, while in my car listening to the radio, the DJ said, "If you want a personal relationship with Jesus Christ and to make Him Lord of your life, pray this with me..."

(I had been praying that God would reveal Himself and couldn't help but wonder if this was Him speaking to me.)

So, I joined the DJ and repeated the following: "Jesus, I surrender my life to You. I believe that You are the Messiah and that You died on the cross for my sins. Please forgive me for all of my sins. Guide and direct me and show me more of who You are. Amen."

"Now, you are 'born again'," the DJ said, and went on to share: "No matter what you've done, your sins have been forgiven." He then quoted:

> [11]*"If we confess our sins,*
> *He is faithful and just to forgive us our sins*
> *and to cleanse us*
> *from all unrighteousness."*

All of a sudden, I felt a sense of relief and I knew that the Lord was touching my heart. I had an encounter with God through Jesus Christ that would change my life forever. I was excited to share this miracle with my husband and children.

Hallelujah!

As I continued reading the Bible, I located other scriptures about [12]following Jesus and about Christ dying for our sins. Here are a few:

*[13]"... If you confess with your mouth
the Lord Jesus and believe in your heart
that God has raised Him from the dead,
you will be saved."*

*[14] "If anyone is in Christ,
he is a new creation;
old things have passed away;
behold, all things have become new."*

*[15]"Most assuredly, I say to you,
he who hears My word
and believes in Him who sent Me
has everlasting life,
and shall not come into judgment,
but has passed from death into life."*

[16]"He who believes in Me has everlasting life."

Rancho Christian Center

It was my desire to belong to a church and prayed that God would lead us to the right one. So, when the kids and I were invited to attend a service at the same church as the Food Pantry where I was volunteering, I knew that I had to check it out.

Since Al used our only car to play tennis on Sundays, the kids and I had to find a ride. I called my friend, Denice, who said that she and her husband, Mike, would be glad to pick us up anytime. It was a pleasure to observe a happily married couple and especially uplifting to meet a man who deeply loved the Lord.

During Rancho Christian Center's service, the pastor quoted from the Bible and shared about how his relationship with Jesus Christ changed his life. He encouraged us to meet with him if we had questions or concerns. At the end, the pastor asked if anyone wanted prayer. I reacted the same way as I did the first time I attended the church's Food Pantry and thought, *"Why wouldn't I want to be prayed for?"* Also, I was having tremendous struggles with my marriage and knew that I needed help.

Denice went with me to the front of the church. A vibrant lady named Bonnie Kramer, who had, in years past, dealt with similar marital issues as mine, prayed for my marriage. It was a comforting and powerful prayer - one which I will never forget. *Years later, Bonnie and her husband, John, became our family's home group leaders.*

I believe that the Lord answered my prayers by leading us to an excellent church and, even though Al wasn't joining us, he relinquished the car so that the kids and I would be able to attend each week.

Getting to church was not easy. Top priority was Lana's health; second, the kids and I needed to be dressed, fed, and out the door. Third, I had to release Lana to a classroom environment which she wasn't used to because she was being home-schooled. Her Sunday school teacher, Angie Coffey, understood Lana's circumstances and was wonderful with her. Alfie enjoyed church and was loved by his teachers - and to top it off, his friend, Travis, was in his classroom.

First Time Homeowner's Program

It was the year 2000. The kids were getting older *(and so was I!)* and I was seriously wondering if we would ever be able to buy a house.

One day, I read about a program which offered first-time homeowners the opportunity to own a home. As long as certain guidelines were followed, the city of Upland would provide the down payment. *What an opportunity - could this be for us?*

Although we were doing okay financially (Al and his friend had developed a screen printing and embroidery business), we still owed money from the time prior to Lana's heart transplant, and in order for us to qualify for this program, we couldn't have any debt.

So, I contacted the collection agencies with the goal of making payment arrangements. To my surprise, OUR DEBT WAS PAID! (You don't hear those words every day!)

Was this a sign from God?

In the Bible, God tells us to make our desires known to Him, so, I prayed that we would find a three-bedroom, two-bathroom house in a safe neighborhood with a backyard and garage.

We met with the program's representatives and turned in the necessary documents. As Al and I drove through every block in Upland looking for our "new" home, we found that either prices weren't in our range, neighborhoods weren't suited for us, or the "perfect home" wasn't for sale. I chuckled, however, because although it seemed impossible that we would actually find a house, I knew that if God wanted us to have this blessing, He would make a way.

Finding us a House

Days later, as the kids and I were leaving for a family function, I jokingly said to Al, "Find us a house while we're gone, okay?" While we were out of town, Al was driving home from the tennis courts and saw an elderly lady watering her lawn. Al got out of the car and asked if she was planning to sell her home. She had a puzzled look on her face and asked, "How did you know? The realtors weren't supposed to disclose that information until this afternoon."

Al told her that he wanted to buy her home. The seller, whose name was Artist, gave Al the real estate agent's phone number, and he made the call. Artist insisted on giving Al a tour of the house, but he said that he didn't need a tour; he knew that this was to be his home.

Al handed the broker two thousand dollars and told the owner and broker that he was ready to purchase the house. He shared that his wife and kids were out of town, but that he would sign a contingency form stating that he would buy the house even if his wife didn't agree. *(He knew that I would love it!)*

While Al was signing the purchase papers, cars lined up outside, along with a person holding a "for sale" sign. Al informed everyone that the house was already being sold and that he was in the process of signing documents. He also told the person who was about to place the "for sale" sign that he didn't want holes in the grass outside his new home.

I will always remember the shaking of my husband's hands as he gave me the stack of papers and said, "You told me to find us a house while you were gone and here it is."

When Al took me to see the house for the first time, I was overjoyed - *All of my prayers from God were answered!*

Will We Have a Home Sweet Home?

We were thrilled to have found our perfect home (which met the city's specifications) and figured that the legalities would easily fall into place. *Not so!* The mortgage broker was dragging his feet which caused us to be concerned that time would run out.

To make matters worse, we found out for the first time that a down payment of eight thousand dollars was needed by the end of the next day, or else the deal would be terminated. We didn't have that kind of money. *Tears filled my eyes.*

One of our family members helped us by covering most of the down payment, and our broker took a reduction in her commissions.

Down to the wire - the very last day - papers were signed. In September of 2000, we bought our beautiful home in Upland, CA, which we're still living in today.

When we first took the kids to see the house, Lana said that she didn't like it. When we asked her the reason, she simply replied, "It isn't pink."

By the way, Lana loves the color pink - as evidenced by her wardrobe, bedroom, and sometimes even her hair!

Another Blessing - Trisha

One of the greatest blessings of living in Upland was a sweet girl named Trisha. Trisha, and her family, lived up the street from us, and Lana and Trisha spent many days in each other's homes. Today, they are still the best of friends - like sisters.

A few years ago, Trisha's family moved away *(a sad time, indeed!)*, but we are so glad that her grandma, Wilma, is still our neighbor, and that we can spend time with Trisha whenever she comes to Upland.

Marriage on the Rocks

The challenges in our lives continued to wreak havoc on our marriage and alcohol was a major problem. I was living in fear and torment and wondered what condition my husband would be in when he came home OR if he would make it home at all.

The kids and I needed to be removed from this environment, so I turned to Al's dad, Alfred. I knew that Alfred had a soft spot in his heart for me - and especially for his granddaughter, Lana - so when I asked if he and his wife, Grandma Adriana, would allow us to move in with them, they graciously said that we could.

It wasn't long before my husband figured out where we were and tried to bring us home. I told Al that we would move back only if he agreed to seek pastoral counsel, so he made an appointment with our church's Pastors David Cunningham and Elver Mendenhall.

After the meeting, Al said that he would work on "giving up the driver's seat" and allowing Jesus to be the pilot. Days following the meeting, a new song came on the radio called, "Jesus, Take the Wheel" (sung by Carrie Underwood), and I felt that this was a message to us from God.

For Valentine's Day that year, I asked my husband for a gift - that he join us for church. On my birthday, I asked for the same gift. After those two times, he attended with us on a regular basis.

Although Al was consuming alcohol less often, he had not fully given up the "wheel" and was still allowing negative influences into his life. I complained, yelled, and tried to come up with things to say that would cause him to change. I was frustrated and discouraged because I knew of Al's wonderful capabilities and wanted so much more for him and for us.

Devastation - Again!

At the end of 2001, a lump appeared on Lana's neck. Antibiotics were prescribed and the lump went away. Weeks later, it returned. We rushed her to the hospital.

At ten years old, Lana was diagnosed with Non-Hodgkin's Lymphoma (malignant cancer cells in the lymph system). Since the lymphoma was intertwined through the carotid artery in her neck, taking out the cancer was not an option.

Cancer was also discovered on Lana's lung.

Even though removing the cancer wasn't possible, it was imperative that certain procedures be done immediately. A biopsy of her neck (to find out if she had Leukemia or any other type of cancer) was essential. Next, a central line (a catheter placed in a large vein in her chest for the purpose of administering medication and drawing blood) had to be surgically placed. Third, a spinal tap (a needle inserted into the spinal canal in order to evaluate the spinal fluid surrounding the brain and spinal cord) was also necessary.

In addition, we felt that it would be wise to have her tonsils and adenoids taken out, and here's why:

Lana's recent MRI and sleep study showed that her brain wasn't getting enough oxygen which resulted in strained sleep. *It would usually take a few hours for Lana to finally fall asleep at night!* So, since Lana had already been scheduled to have her tonsils and adenoids removed in the upcoming weeks, we decided to include this with all of her other procedures.

Lana was a severely weakened state, so Al and I firmly requested that Lana be given anesthesia only once, which meant that FOUR PROCEDURES WOULD BE DONE AT THE SAME TIME! Doctors were in agreement.

Times were ridiculously HARD! My brain and body were tired! I kept focusing on staying strong and not showing sadness or fear to Lana.

Many hours later, Lana came out of surgery. After having had a biopsy, the insertion of a central line, a spinal tap, and the removal of her tonsils and adenoids, she asked for a hamburger and french fries! The nurse was shocked at Lana's request and called the doctor to ask if this would be okay. By the time the doctor approved, I had already made the purchase and Lana had consumed the whole burger and fries (minus the crispy parts) and was full and content!

Lana now had a central line which forced her to sleep on her back. The line needed daily checking and cleaning. It was scary because two hoses were protruding from her chest, and if the hoses were pulled, she would be in a life threatening situation.

Even with everything going on, LANA DIDN'T COMPLAIN! She was the happiest and most pleasant patient ever. She loved the attention and was treated like royalty at the hospital. *One of her doctors even brought her sushi for dinner!*

One time when Dr. Hohl, Lana's orthopedic doctor, told her that if she didn't do her leg exercises, she would need surgery, she told him, "I like surgery."

Heart transplant and cancer doctors worked together to establish the appropriate blend of medication for Lana. This was a challenge. The higher the dose of heart medicine, the weaker Lana's immune system would be, but in order to fight the cancer, Lana had to have powerful medication and a strong immune system.

It was a "Catch 22" - a seemingly impossible situation - with a dismal prognosis.

Dr. Liesl Mathias, Lana's gifted oncologist, knew a doctor who had been successfully treating a young patient with a similar medical history to Lana. Although experimental, this program had been successful thus far, so we agreed that following this plan would be the best idea.

I turned to these words from the Bible which gave me comfort while going through this DREADFUL STORM:

> [17]*"Come to Me, all you who labor*
> *and are heavy burdened,*
> *and I will give you rest."*
>
> [18]*"Peace I leave with you,*
> *My peace I give to you;*
> *not as the world gives do I give to you.*
> *Let not your heart be troubled,*
> *neither let it be afraid."*

Lana's veins were so small and so damaged that getting blood was difficult and painful. During an especially awful time when the venipuncturist had already made two unsuccessful attempts at drawing Lana's blood, one of our pastors came to see Lana. Pastor Bob prayed as the nurse was finally able to draw blood. He sat quietly in Lana's room with me and was a wonderful blessing during a really tough time.

During Wednesday and Sunday services, our church members would stand in a large circle as they held hands and prayed for Lana. Family, friends, and our church family from around the world, were praying.

I was clinging to the following words (which became Lana's favorite Bible verse):

> [19]*"With men this is impossible, but with God all things are possible."*

As I placed my hand on Lana's neck and prayed for God to save my daughter, I witnessed the lump on Lana's neck disappear. When the next CT scan was performed, the spot on her lung was also miraculously GONE!

Lana's prognosis which had originally been deemed "terminal" was now not looking so terminal! She was given a treatment plan under the category of "preventative."

Lana was released, on an out-patient basis, with a central line connected to an artery in her heart. She was amazing! At ten years old, she was cleaning her lines and changing her own bandages. She even designed a method of attaching the lines to a bikini top and then covering the lines with a shirt. We walked around the cancer ward as she shared this discovery with other patients.

Lana was receiving chemotherapy treatments every three weeks, along with frequent testing and doctor visits. She experienced severe headaches, body aches, hair loss, and weight gain. Despite her situation, Lana had a wonderful attitude.

Clumps of hair gathered on her comb, until she calmly said, "Mom, just cut it off." She eventually lost all of her hair, but it didn't disturb her. I told her, "You're still beautiful," to which she replied, "I know." When I explained that her hair would grow back and that it could be different, i.e., thicker, curlier, etc., she said that she wanted it to come back "pink." *(When Lana's hair finally grew back, our favorite hair stylist and friend, Anna Marie Belk, dyed her hair pink.)*

For Christmas that year, Lana's "High-5" group from church came to the house and surprised her with bags of gifts. In spite of a massive headache, Lana jumped up to spend time with her friends. When I checked on the girls, I found them in the bathroom polishing each other's nails!

After six LONG and CHALLENGING months, Lana was released with a cancer-free bill of health. *Hallelujah!*

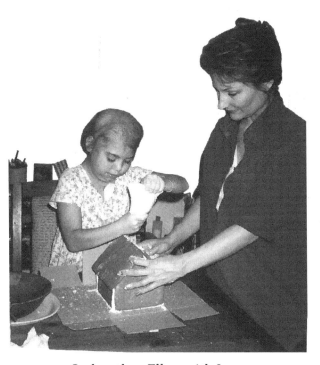

Godmother Ellen with Lana
during cancer treatments

Painting nails with friends - 2001

My Marriage - To Survive or To Fail

Our marriage was in constant turmoil. I
was struggling - with the relationship my
husband had with alcohol - and with the
person I had become. I spent day after
day yelling, nagging, and complaining,
but nothing seemed to change. In the
middle of all of that, I was raising and
home-schooling children, monitoring health
issues, and attempting to take care of
day-to-day "life".

I needed help, so I met with my pastor who
gently informed me that I was "enabling" my
husband and that I was part of the problem,
but not part of the solution.

*How can I be part of the problem when
I'm not the one making the destructive
choices?*

With my voice raised, I cried out, "I hate
the word [20]'enabler'," but soon came to
realize that Pastor Dave had been right.
I wasn't sure how I was to change my

behavior, but I knew that I had to keep my focus on the Lord, no matter what was going on around me.

I had recently read about [27]"fasting" from the Old and New Testament and the miracles that the Lord performed during those times. I also remembered that my dear friend, Ellen, fasted for forty days while praying that God would heal Lana's cancer.

Could Ellen's fasting have had anything to do with Lana's miraculous healing?

Willing to try anything, I made a seemingly irrational decision to go on a two-week fast. I believed that the sacrifice of not eating could help to save my marriage, so even though I didn't fully understand the concept, I followed what I believed the Lord wanted me to do.

I was praying and talking with God. I felt a tugging on my heart to forgive my husband, but didn't feel that he deserved forgiveness for all that he had put us through. The voice in my head (which I later came to discover was the Holy Spirit) asked if I felt that I deserved forgiveness for all of my mistakes. "No," was my reply. It was then that I realized (and found Bible verses about this) that if I wanted [22] God to forgive me, I needed to also forgive others. So, I made the choice to forgive my husband for everything. Then, I confessed to Al and to the Lord that I hadn't been a kind, loving, or respectful wife and that I came into the marriage with many flaws and dysfunctions. I also repented to God, in the name of Jesus, for how I had treated my family and for everything I'd ever done which had not been pleasing to Him.

During the two week fasting period (which was no "cake walk"), I would ask the Lord things like, "How am I supposed to ignore the 'elephant' (referring to the alcohol situation) in the middle of my living room (that I keep running over) and its affect on my family?" I was upset and confused. *Could I ever truly love my husband again?*

So, with all of the faith I could muster up, I prayed that I would have a greater love for my husband than ever before and that I would see Al as God sees him.

The small voice in my head, [23](the Holy Spirit) began to guide me as to when to talk to Al. I would no longer nag or yell, but would speak in a calm voice.

In the midst of expecting the Lord to change my husband, I found that it was ME who was being transformed. I was developing a deeper love for Al than I had ever dreamed possible - *I was seeing him through the eyes of God!*

Al was still making the choice to drink, and I was making the choice to turn to God. When Al would come home intoxicated, I would read from the Bible (out loud) until he went to bed. Christian music filled our home as I sang and prayed. I also turned to Christian mentors for prayer and guidance. I relied on the Lord to help me - and help me He did!

"I am dedicating my marriage to You, and asking that You heal and bless it," is what I said to the Lord. I didn't know how He would fulfill this deep desire of my heart (this is where faith came in), but I prayed and declared that He would perform this miracle.

Many among my family and friends didn't understand or agree with my decision to stay with Al (and I didn't blame them for feeling that way); however, I needed to follow what I felt God wanted me to do.

I was becoming empowered by a presence that could not have come from me. Even though I was still in the midst of a storm, my "feelings" were no longer controlled by the circumstances. I felt a "supernatural" peace that I had never experienced before. I recognized this as the same type of peace that I had observed in my friends Janice, Cheryl, Ellen, Mike, and Denice.

My Mom

The following year after Al's father died of lung cancer, my mom was also diagnosed with cancer. This was shocking, because my mom had always been healthy and had taken excellent care of herself.

During Mom's last months, my brother and I went to Las Vegas often to see our parents. Devin and I used to talk about how difficult it was to be around them, but also how difficult it was to be away. Watching our parents endure this emotional and physical pain was nearly unbearable.

Near the end, I apologized to my mom about having been a difficult child. She forgave me and said that she understood that I was just trying to "find my way." Then, she said that she was sorry that she hadn't been able to open up and to "be herself" until now.

Although I wish that we would have communicated those words earlier, I was comforted that we were able to forgive and to share a precious, but difficult moment.

In September of 2005, Mom passed away. This was a deep loss for me, as my mom and I talked nearly every day for most of my life. We had much love and respect for each other and I knew that, no matter what, she was in my corner. All these years later, I think about her all the time and miss her dearly.

My parents had celebrated their forty-eighth anniversary one week prior to Mom's death; they had been in love for all of those years. Watching my dad suffer was especially awful for my brother and me.

Mom's passing was heartbreaking for Lana. Lana's grandmother (who Lana called "Mom") loved and understood Lana in a way that no one else did. She taught Lana how to knit, paint, make pizza and chocolate covered strawberries, and create many neat crafts.

Whenever my parents came to visit, they would bring bags of clothes and presents. When we went to see them in Vegas, they would have "cool" projects for the kids to do, and would take them to fun places like Circus Circus. One of my greatest memories was witnessing the love that my parents had for my children.

"Nana," who was ninety-five at the time, suffered tremendous heartache, because my mother was her only daughter and best friend. Before Mom passed away, my grandmother cried out to God, "Please, take me instead."

As I sought to understand why my mother died so painfully, I realized that I may never know the answer.

I believe with all my heart that God is GOOD and God is LOVE, and that many things happen that are not a part of His original plan.

Cruelty, sickness, cancer, heart infirmities, and all diseases are the result of sin which came into the world when Adam and Eve disobeyed God. This was not God's original plan when He created us.

I heard my mom speak to the Lord many times during her last days. She would say, "God, help me - oh, I know - You are!"

The Bible says that [24]we will find Him when we seek Him with all of our hearts.

She knew that God was with her during her time of need and that it was God's desire for her to [25]be in heaven with Him.

Tympanic Plasty

Lana suffered many ear infections throughout her young life due to tiny ear canals. As a child, she wanted so badly to learn to swim, so I would enroll her in classes, but each time, she wouldn't be able to complete the class due to another infection. Tubes were placed in her ears, but soon after, they became contaminated and had to be removed.

Years later, Doctor Rowe and Doctor Stewart (Lana's awesome ear, nose and throat doctors) recommended that the bone in Lana's eardrum be cut down.

My mom had passed away days before, so this would be the first time that Lana would endure surgery without her "Mom." My mom had been involved in Lana's medical situations and would communicate daily with Al whenever Lana was in the hospital. My parents were always concerned and supportive. We all especially missed Mom during this time.

"Tympanic Plasty" surgery was performed on Lana (at age fifteen), but she was still getting ear infections. Drops and antibiotics were prescribed regularly, and although Lana's doctors were wonderful, there wasn't anything else they could do.

I would often pray over her ears that God would perform a miracle - and, one day, it happened - The Lord healed Lana from ear infections. *Hallelujah!*

Coronary Artery Disease

Dreadful news came our way in the beginning of 2007 when Lana was diagnosed with Coronary Artery Disease. We had hoped and prayed that her first heart transplant (in 1992) would last a lifetime, but that wasn't the case. Lana's heart was failing and, at sixteen years of age, she needed a second heart transplant. *Oh, these were painful words to hear!*

We were called in to discuss Lana's options. After a strong recommendation from Dr. Chinnock, the wonderful man who had been Lana's heart doctor for nearly her whole life, we agreed to the transplant.

We sent Lana out of the room to ask the doctor some questions. When Lana came back, Dr. Chinnock asked her, "Do you know what we were talking about?" "Yeah, my new heart transplant," Lana said. "How do you feel about that?" asked the doctor. "Well," said Lana, "I don't want to have a new heart." Dr. Chinnock said, "I don't want you to have one either, but you need to have it so that you can be healthy," to which Lana replied, "Okay, let's do it already."

To be placed on the heart transplant list *(again)*, Lana had to undergo numerous tests and procedures, including EEG's, EKG's, blood work, an MRI, dental work, x-rays, a PET scan, and more. It seemed that whenever she would complete a test, a new one would be scheduled, and although these tests were uncomfortable, painful, and time consuming, Lana was much like a "soldier" and bravely did what needed to be done - with a smile *(most of the time)*!

On April 30, 2007, it was official - Lana was on the heart transplant list.

Heart Transplant List

"Keep your cell phones on, have your bags packed, and be ready to go when you get our call," is what we were told.

We had to stay close to home, and every time the phone rang - day or night, we jumped. *Was this the hospital? Was this the time?*

It was a challenge to stay positive and to not live in fear. When thoughts would come, like: *"What if a heart doesn't get here in time,"* and *"What if she doesn't survive the surgery,"* I needed to turn to God more than ever.

So, we waited *(somewhat patiently)* and continued to pray for God's will to be done in Lana's life.

The Call

After being on the heart transplant list for nine weeks, on July 6, 2007, at six-thirty in the morning, the phone rang: "A heart is ready for Lana." We were told that the heart was coming from a twenty-year-old who had a car accident and was now without brain activity.

I hung up the phone and cried and prayed for that young lady and her family.

There aren't enough words to express the gratitude we will always have toward this family for sacrificing their child's body to be a gift of life for someone they had never met. To me, this incredible act of love is a reminder of what God did when He allowed His only Son to die so that we could have eternal life.

We stopped by church to pray with our pastors and then headed to Loma Linda. Though we were overflowing with emotion, we trusted that God had it under control and was taking care of everything.

Alfie's friend (and my godson) Travis had spent the night. The next morning (while Travis was still at our house), is when the "heart transplant call" came in. Travis was part of our home-school program, so I often taught him along with my kids. Since the three of them had completed their school work for the week - and we had no plans for the next day - they were allowed to stay up as late as they wanted.

Little did I know that the "next day" would be spent at the hospital receiving a new heart for Lana.

(It worked out well because the boys were so tired that they fell asleep on the hospital floor!)

Lana, while on the list for her second heart transplant in 2007, did not allow her challenges to control her positive outlook on life.

Heart Transplant Number Two!

Lana didn't care for Loma Linda's hospital attire, so she designed her own: "Pink" material with "pink" buttons, "pink" velcro, and even a "pink" pocket which held small hospital equipment. Sally Weber, our talented and creative friend, made Lana's hospital gown and it was beautiful, original, and approved by the doctors! Sally also made a pajama set for Lana's days following surgery.

When we arrived at the hospital, we were approached by Lana's surgeon, Dr. Anees Razzouk, who prayed that her surgery would be successful and that God's hand would be upon the entire procedure.

We were overwhelmed - how many surgeons actually pray for their patient prior to surgery?!

We expected to wait many hours, but instead, Lana was rushed in for one last x-ray, and before we knew it, she was being wheeled into the operating room. I kissed her on the cheek, and with a big smile on her face, Lana waved "good-bye." She had to be the most content, confident, and joyful person to ever receive a second heart transplant in heart transplant history!

I, on the other hand, was an emotional mess.

However, we chose not to live in fear, but rather to appreciate whatever time the Lord would allow us to have with our daughter. My husband would say, "It's a win-win situation. If the Lord takes her, we'll be grateful that she will be pain-free in heaven; if He allows her to remain, we will be thrilled to have more time with her!"

The Bible says,

> [26]*"For if we live, we live to the Lord,*
> *and if we die, we die to the Lord.*
> *Therefore, whether we live or die,*
> *we are the Lord's."*

While Lana was in surgery, our pastor and friends came to the hospital. As we prayed together, I had a vision of Jesus holding Lana's new heart in His hands. I believe that God showed me: "She's going to be okay." Even though I didn't know what "okay" meant, I was experiencing a supernatural peace that could only come from Him - and I was comforted!

Still, waiting was a challenge, and since we had lots of time, I went into the chaplain's office and had a long conversation with the Lord. While praying for my daughter, I had as much peace as a mother can have during a time like this.

Finally, finally, finally - on July 6, 2007 at eleven-thirty at night, Lana's second heart transplant was complete. At age sixteen, Lana now had a new heart.

It took nearly six hours to remove the heart from her first transplant. *(Her heart had been in the same position for over fifteen years and didn't want to come out!)*

As Dr. Razzouk and his surgical team left Lana's room, we witnessed the group's exhaustion as they were hunched over and could barely stand. *My husband and I will always be grateful for the doctors and staff who worked so hard to perform our daughter's surgery!*

Lana was in the ICU with twenty-four hour private nursing care. We were permitted in Lana's room for only a few minutes each hour. This was awful because we wanted to be with our daughter every moment.

Al and I took turns cat-napping in very uncomfortable chairs that night.

The Month From _ _ _ _!

Following is a personal diary that I kept during the thirty days following Lana's second heart transplant:

<u>July 7:</u> It is two o'clock in the morning - Two and a half hours after Lana's second heart transplant - and Lana is awake. The specialists test her to see if she can breathe without the breathing tube, but according to the equipment (much more advanced than what was used on Lana during her first heart transplant fifteen years ago); Lana would not be able to breathe without the tube. When I enter the room, Lana looks at me (while the tube is inside her throat) and motions with her mouth: "I can breathe!"

Lana Can Do It!

I tell Lana that I will be right back and follow the specialists down the hall to ask them to please remove the breathing tube. *(I am nice at first.)* They inform me that they had just tested her and that breathing on her own would not be possible at this time.

Since I trust my daughter who showed me that she can breathe without help, again I ask the specialists *(not as nice this time)* to remove the tube. Against their wishes and expertise, they take out the tube and Lana is able to breathe on her own. The technicians are amazed.

July 8: Lana is awake all day - she's happy, joyful, and on morphine. Dad brings her steak and sushi for dinner. *Life is good!*

July 9: Excruciating pain sets in. The doctors want her to get out of bed, as pneumonia is a serious threat. Screaming all the way, she finally walks a little and then lies on the floor and says, "NO MORE!" X-rays are taken, and it's discovered that, as a result of removing her former heart, Lana's spine is crooked.

This explains the horrendous pain!

Fluid is in her lungs. Doctors and nurses tell her that if she doesn't walk, she will wind up with pneumonia.

They also tell us that they will no longer be giving her morphine, but that Tylenol will be okay. Al and I STRONGLY explain that the medicine will not be powerful enough, so they compromise and agree on Vicodin (or Hydrocodine).

I feel like screaming as I witness my sweet daughter in agony. I tell myself that I must be strong and I must keep it together. Please, Lord, help me!

July 10: Blood sugar levels are going up and down due to the strong intravenous heart medication and, although she doesn't have diabetes, she now has diabetes-type symptoms. I get trained to administer "finger-poking" (which they want done every hour), and even though Lana abhors needles, she's glad that I am the one to perform this task.

I also learn how to give insulin (and have to practice by giving myself a shot - yuk!), but pray that I don't ever have to do this on Lana!

Her lungs are still filled with fluid and she must continue to cough and to walk.

It hurts - A LOT. *It hurts me and her dad, too - A LOT!* Dad brings her steak for dinner.

July 11: It is awful, but I am poking her finger every hour (eighteen hours straight) and insulin is being given as needed (not yet by me!).

There's still a lot of fluid in her lungs, so they remove one of the three chest tubes, which is supposed to take away some of her pain. It doesn't do anything. *I feel horrible! If I could trade places with my daughter, I surely would!*

July 12: A biopsy is performed with results coming in tomorrow. The second chest tube is removed, but this doesn't alleviate the pain either.

They're talking about releasing her tomorrow. *WHAT - SO SOON? Her heart transplant was only a week ago. She has a chest tube, congestion, a nasty looking chest x-ray, unstable blood sugar levels, and is still in a great deal of pain. This doesn't make sense to me.*

July 13: The final chest tube is taken out. Paperwork is being completed, and, although it seems too soon, we are thrilled to be going home. We say our "good-byes" and check out of the Ronald McDonald House (where we have been staying in order to be near the hospital).

It is one of the worst nights of our lives. Lana is up all night coughing and Al and I are up all night fighting. Lana was released from the hospital too early and we now need to return.

<u>July 14:</u> First thing in the morning, we pack our bags and our son and head back to Loma Linda - our "home away from home!"

After spending an uncomfortable and frustrating ELEVEN HOURS IN THE EMERGENCY ROOM, Lana is diagnosed with pneumonia. She has a high fever and the x-ray is worse than the day before.

At ten-thirty at night, she is FINALLY admitted back into her SAME room in the intensive care unit. Everything has to be re-done, including a new IV and all of the other "hook-ups" from yesterday. Since we lost our spot at the Ronald McDonald House, we now have to drive back and forth from home to the hospital each day.

It would have been SO much easier and less traumatic had we stayed in the hospital instead of being released TOO SOON and spending one horrific night at home!

Recently, I heard the following song which sums up how I was feeling at the time. The [27] singer is speaking to God as she sings:

> *"Standing on a road I didn't plan*
> *Wondering how I got to where I am*
> *I'm trying to hear that still-small-voice*
> *I'm trying to hear above the noise.*

*Though I walk through the shadows
And I am so afraid.*

*I get so tired of holding on
I can't let go; I can't move on.
I want to believe there's meaning here.*

*Please stay please stay right beside me
With every single step I take.*

*How many times have You heard me cry out,
'God please take this'
How many times have You given me strength
to just keep breathing.*

Oh, I need you. God, I need You now."

July 15: A bacterial infection is discovered in her blood. She is now on powerful intravenous antibiotics.

July 16: A tube is placed into her body *(again)* and excess fluid is removed. Lana discovers that there's oozing and an infection under her stitches. The stitches have to be cut open and the tissue underneath must be delicately cleansed. Lana is in a great deal of pain.

July 17: After being poked by needles for many days, Lana's blood sugar levels are now good. I ask to speak to a doctor, but the doctor isn't available, so, my husband and I make the decision to end Lana's unnecessary pain by stopping the needles.

Days later, when the doctor finally arrives, he is upset with us for making this decision without him, but is in agreement that Lana no longer needs to be tested. Lana calls this "our fight" ... *some battles are worth fighting!*

July 18: The tube attached to her lungs is removed - *hallelujah!* The doctor cleans out the infection beneath her stitches. Lana is still in pain, especially when she coughs or walks. Grandpa (my dad) comes from Vegas to visit and brings her steak for dinner.

July 19: Her current IV must be removed and replaced with a new one. It is crucial that Lana have her intravenous medication, so when the technician is unable to get the needle in, I ask if there is someone else who may be better qualified. *(I don't want Lana to have to go through more pain than is absolutely necessary.)* Although the doctor says that no one else is available, a blessing happens and a new person shows up who easily inserts the IV needle. *Thank you, Lord!*

We are informed that Lana now needs to have a "PICC Line." *I have never heard of this, so I am petrified.* The nurse tells me that a "PICC Line" is a tube (or catheter) that is surgically inserted into a large vein in Lana's arm and then guided up into the main vein near Lana's heart. She says that having this will make it easier to give medication and draw blood and will last longer than the IV's.

WHAT IF THEY'RE UNABLE TO DO THIS? Lana's veins have been traumatized for so long, and I'm SUPER concerned that inserting this tube will be nearly impossible. AND, if this procedure doesn't work, the alternative is that she will have to receive IV's every two days for who knows how long - her veins cannot handle that!

First attempt - FAILURE. Second attempt - FAILURE. The doctor tells us that this doesn't look promising. As I agonizingly witness an attempt to place the PICC Line in her vein for the THIRD AND LAST TIME, I pray and ask God to perform a miracle. The PICC Line is FINALLY inserted and I'm able to breathe again. *Praise the Lord!*

What a traumatic and awful day!

July 20: The infection under her stitches must be drained - AGAIN - so the doctor hooks her up to a machine so that some of the fluid can be removed.

An infectious disease doctor comes in to talk with my husband. Lana has severe pneumonia and is being placed on another powerful antibiotic. The x-ray looks worse than ever before.

I am physically and emotionally exhausted and can barely stand. I call my friend, Ellen, who prays for miracles and strength for us.

July 21: After taking blood, it is discovered that Lana has a low white blood cell count and needs a blood transfusion.

We bring Alfie in to spend time with his sister. He tells Lana, "I can't wait to play soccer with you when you get out of the hospital." Alfie begins to sob, as he doesn't know if she will be able to play soccer again or even if she will recover. We rush him out of the room, because we don't want Lana to see this. *It is a very difficult time for the whole family!*

July 22: Another surgery has to be done in order to drain her lungs. This is supposed to take forty-five minutes, but has now taken over three hours. Fear and panic begin to overtake me.

As I am waiting - and waiting - and waiting - for what seems to be an eternity - I turn on the radio and hear the following lyrics:

> [28]*"I'm waiting on You Lord, but it is painful. I'm waiting on You Lord, but it's not easy. But faithfully, I will wait."*

I feel as though this is a message from the Lord that He understands and is with me through these hard times.

FINALLY, Lana's surgery is complete. The nurses apologize for not letting me know sooner that the procedure would take hours longer than expected. *All is good - for the moment.*

July 23: A biopsy is scheduled for tomorrow. This is distressing because Dr. Kuhn, a wonderful surgeon who has always performed these tests on Lana, will not be available.

July 24: We try to postpone the biopsy in order to wait for Dr. Kuhn's return, but the doctors want it done NOW. Heart rejection is common at this point and they want to know that she is in the clear.

The surgeon will have to enter through her groin which will require Lana to remain on her back for six hours following surgery. *I am dreading this!*

Surgery is short and over. To our pleasant surprise, the biopsy is performed through her neck and not the groin. We believe this to be a miracle from God!

July 25: Nurses tell us that Lana will be going home tomorrow. But WAIT...results from her recent biopsy are in. Lana's HEART IS REJECTING.

New medication is started and blood sugar levels must be checked regularly.   Twice tonight, she gets insulin shots! *HERE WE GO AGAIN!*

July 26: In order for Lana to go home - whenever that is - I must be qualified to do the following: Administer IV medication and insulin shots, take blood sugar levels, change the dressing, pack and clean the opening from the infection beneath her scar, and monitor her heart and blood pressure.

I am not a nurse and I don't want to do any of this. I am fearful that if I'm unable to do something correctly, I will be responsible for my daughter's death. I must not think this way and must focus on the task(s) at hand! I will not allow fear to take over!

July 27: Lana is still on anti-rejection medicine - still receiving blood sugar pokes - still getting insulin shots - and we are still praying for a miracle!

July 28: Freedom! Lana is released on an out-patient basis, but has to go in for check-ups and testing every couple of days. We are blessed to be able to again stay at the Ronald McDonald House. This way, we are close to the hospital and don't have to travel back and forth from home.

Our room at the Ronald McDonald House is filled with a variety of medical supplies and medications, along with an IV machine. I *(with Lana's help!)* am giving IV medication twice a day - *scary!* We are also changing her dressing and packing and cleaning her scar twice a day. In the middle of all of that, blood sugar levels must be checked and recorded four times a day.

Lana is helping with every procedure, as she knows how to do all of this.

It is time for her post-midnight blood sugar level and I'm nervous because this is the time that her numbers are usually high, and when this happens, insulin must be given. I have never given my daughter a shot of insulin, so I pray to God that I won't have to do this now - or ever.

Unfortunately, as suspected, Lana's level is high. I pray again as I make a phone call to the nurse. After being placed on hold for what seems to be an eternity, the voice on the other end of the phone says, "Let's wait until morning and see if the number decreases."

No insulin shot tonight - the Lord answers my prayer!

July 29-30: Morning is here and as we hoped (and prayed), Lana's blood sugar levels normalize and no insulin shot is needed. *Thank you, Jesus!*

Lana's back, neck, and chest are in pain. Medicine helps a little.

July 31-August 1: Blood isn't coming out of her PICC line, which could create a huge problem.

August 2: She is not feeling well and she is VERY tired.

August 3-4: Tonight is the final dose of IV medication. The infection under her scar is healed and we don't have to pack or cleanse the area anymore. *Yeah!*

August 5: Tomorrow Lana is scheduled for an echocardiogram and blood work. I am praying that the technician is able to get blood from her PICC line. Al and Alfie go to church while I stay with Lana.

August 6: The PICC line works and blood tests are complete! We meet with the infectious disease doctor who says that the infection under her scar looks good. Thank the Lord!

Another biopsy *(yuk!)* is scheduled for tomorrow, but…oops… her paperwork is missing. The surgery is rescheduled for August 21. *Maybe this break is a blessing from the Lord!*

August 7: Antibiotics are complete and we are heading home - to our own beds!

<u>August 8:</u> I wake up in utter amazement that I survived the last thirty days and that the four of us are FINALLY HOME!

What Now?

Following her second heart transplant, Lana suddenly developed a crooked spine. Whenever she attempted to stand up, pain would set in. Doctors could do nothing to change it. We knew that the healing of her back could only come from the Lord.

A Miracle!

Years later, x-rays showed that the top of her spine had shifted to the left, while the bottom of her spine shifted to the right, thereby causing her back to be even. *I believe that this can only happen by the grace of God!*

Prayer for Lana Throughout the World!

It brought us great comfort to know that while Lana was undergoing her second heart transplant (and recovery), our church family in the United States and around the world (through Rancho International Ministries ("RIM") was praying and crying out to the Lord for help and healing. We will forever be grateful to our brothers and sisters in Christ and to everyone else who stood with us and prayed for Lana!

My Nana

Three days after we came home from
Loma Linda, we got the call that my
grandmother was in the hospital; she had
stopped eating and wasn't doing well.
When Lana and I went to see her, I said
to Nana, "When Jesus comes for you, go
to Him." She said, "Well, I don't see Him
yet." I said, "You will." Right after that,
she became incoherent and two days later,
at age ninety-seven, she passed away.

Nana was one of my treasured blessings.
For much of my life, especially after my
mom died, Nana and I spoke often -
sometimes several times a day! For years,
Nana celebrated Christmas with us at the
home of our good friends, The Blazy's.
One New Year's Eve, Nana joined us for a
"karaoke night" at our home with friends.

A highlight of Nana's life was her relationship
with Lana, who was eighty years her youn
ger. Nana spent as much time as she could
with her great-granddaughter (even if it
meant taking the bus to do so), and Lana

cherished those times with her "Nana."

Every year on Valentine's Day, Nana would remind me of the blessing that we received on that day in 1992 when Lana returned home from the hospital after receiving her first heart transplant.

Throughout the years, I often spoke to Nana about Jesus and shared passages with her from the Bible. She came to one of our church services, and would have come more often had she been able. I believe that she came to know Jesus as her Messiah and that she accepted Him into her heart during her last moments.

I picture Nana dancing in heaven - she loved to dance. Though I miss her, I know that she's having a wonderful time in her pain-free body!

Graduation from Home-Schooling

Home-schooling Lana and Alfie through the end of high school was one of my greatest joys - and challenges. Besides teaching and dealing with medical stuff, I was helping my husband with his business. It was a continual juggling act AND the house was usually a disaster, but spending quality time with my kids made it all worth it!

The principal at [29]Gorman Learning Center once told me that his favorite students were those who were gifted and those who were in special education programs. I was proud to have one of each!

Alfie was academically advanced and was in the "GATE" (Gifted and Talented Education) program at Gorman. Lana was placed in special education programs, and although physical issues were a constant challenge, she worked hard to do her best.

In 2010, Lana and Alfie graduated high school together. This was such a special day for us (even though Lana was battling pneumonia!). We looked back at the emotional and medical struggles that we endured during these school years and thanked the Lord for allowing us to get to this place.

To add to this wonderful blessing, Alfie received the Salutatorian Award (graduating with a 4.04 grade point average) and was chosen to give a speech to Gorman's graduating class, which included their friends Travis, Emily, Tony, Andrew, and guests.

It was a joy to share the day with our family and friends. I only wish my mom, grandmother, and Al's dad could have been there to celebrate with us!

Another Surgery -
I'm Getting Too Old for This!

Lana had ear surgery when she was fifteen, but now, after eleven years, in 2016, the bone in her ear had grown, causing her eardrum to again be blocked. Discussions with Dr. Stewart, Lana's excellent ENT doctor, led us to believe that opening up her eardrum again would be a wise decision.

We placed Lana on our church's prayer chain and attempted to get a little rest prior to "surgery day." We had to be at the hospital at five o'clock in the morning. All was dark, and I could feel the intense pounding of my heart. Memories of her previous surgeries haunted me and fear and panic began to creep in.

Is she going to make it? Will this be the surgery which will take her out? What condition will she be in when she wakes up ... if she wakes up? I prayed and asked God to help me to not give attention to those negative feelings.

God's presence was with us throughout the day and I knew that Lana was in His hands.

The surgery was successful but Lana was uncomfortable and irritable. She woke up with a swollen face and a bandage around her head. *It is awful seeing my daughter that way!*

We were glad to be able to take her home. Even though she was in pain, Lana put on her swollen "game face" while her godmother, Ellen, spent the day watching movies and eating lunch with her (and me).

What's Happening These Days?

It is now 2018, and I have been working on this book for nearly three years. Every time I pick up a page, I find something that needs to be changed and I wonder: WILL THE BOOK EVER BE DONE? I guess if you're reading this, it must be finished!

Eighteen years ago, I made the most important decision of my life by accepting Jesus Christ as my Lord and Savior. Today, I do my best to lead a life which focuses on God's love, mercy, grace, and forgiveness.

> [30]*"And whatever you do in word or deed,*
> *do all in the name of the Lord Jesus,*
> *giving thanks to God the Father*
> *through Him."*

This year marks the fourteenth time I have read the entire Bible *(second best decision!)*. To me, the Bible is more than a history, science, or theology book - it is the written word of God which provides me with inner peace and strength every time

I pick it up. My morning ritual is to drink a delicious cup of coffee *(I make the best coffee!)* while reading about the Lord and developing a closer relationship with Him.

I am blessed with an awesome family - I'm married to a wonderful and devoted husband who loves Jesus, me, and our children. Al has a great sense of humor and brings the light of the Lord with him wherever he goes. He is highly intelligent and intuitive and supports me in every area of our lives.

Thank you, God, for healing my marriage and for loving my husband - even more than I do!

I am a proud mom who has a hard time believing that her beautiful children are now adults.

My son, Alfie, is a kind and compassionate Christian young man who has a heart for people. Alfie and I often go out for meals and have done this since he was a child. I value these times and am honored that, at twenty-six, my son still enjoys spending time with his mom!

The other day when Alfie and I were at a restaurant, his cell phone rang. I questioned who was on the phone, since the call was interrupting our time, and Alfie responded, "No one." I asked, "So, is 'no one' more important than me?" He answered, "Yes, 'no one' is more important than you, Mom." *What a sweetheart!*

The relationship between Alfie and Lana is different from the one that they had as children. Up until their teen-age years, they were best friends. Due to physical and mental challenges, Lana hasn't grown up as quickly as Alfie. So, even though she would want her brother "back," and he, too, misses their closeness, the bond is no longer there. Still, they have a strong love for each other and there isn't anything Alfie wouldn't do for his sister! Whenever she asks to spend time with him, he does his best to make himself available for her. Alfie refers to Lana as his "super hero."

Lana, who is now twenty-eight years old, is the kindest person I have ever had the pleasure to know. She continues to teach me about patience, tenderness, forgiveness, and love for people.

It has been twenty-six years since her first heart transplant, seventeen years since she had cancer, and eleven years since her second transplant. *Praise the Lord!*

Since Lana's immune system is fragile, she must do her best to keep away from germs. This is challenging because she wants to participate in many things, like "Awana," church, and any activity where she can be around friends and family. Sometimes Lana says, "I wish I could be like other people." While it is painful to hear my daughter say those things, I tell her how special she is and how she has enriched the lives of so many people (like her boyfriend, Allen).

Then, when she's not looking, I cry!

Another challenging situation has to do with her peers. Lana has developed slower than those of her age (probably due to prior strokes and/or Spinal Meningitis), so friends will often leave her behind and move on to new relationships. Lana doesn't bring this up often, but I know that it disturbs her greatly.

Rancho Christian Center has been my family's church for the past eighteen years. It has been a joy and an honor to have a wonderful "church family" and to run the church's Food Pantry (along with an awesome team, including Stella, Beverly, Melissa, Ron, Frank, Pattie, Jennifer, Lana, and Virginia). I also teach Jr. High Sunday School to a super bunch of kids (including Lana), assist with various church events, and help my friend, Ellen, as she leads our Home Group.

Christmas is significant to me, for without Christ, there would be no Christmas. We celebrate with the BEST fresh tree (chosen by my husband), beautiful decorations (including popcorn strung together many years ago when Lana was four months old), gifts, and a delicious meal shared with special friends, like Beverly and Howard.

What's New Year's Eve without friends, hats, necklaces, noise-blowers, snacks, and, of course, karaoke? Well, that's what happens at our home on the last night of each year!

After my mom died, I prayed that my dad would find someone special with whom to spend the rest of his life. I knew that this would take a miracle since he had been so in love with his wife. Well, God answered the prayer, and Marlene, a beautiful and lively lady, joined our family.

My dad and Marlene had a fabulous marriage until cancer sadly took Marlene's life (during the writing of this book) in March of 2017. It was awful watching my dad go through the pain of losing the second love of his life!

We visit my dad in Las Vegas at every opportunity, especially during Thanksgiving when my brother, Devin, and his wife, Patricia (who I'm proud to have as my sister-in-law), join us while dad sings "Bless This House" (a tradition since I was little).

Life has been challenging, difficult,

wonderful, blessed, sad, scary, joyful, and full of surprises. Without the Lord's help, I would have most likely lost my sanity. It's comforting to know that God is always with me, even during the most painful of storms! Obviously, I don't know what the future holds, but I know that every day brings my family and me one step closer to our ultimate home in Paradise!

The Bible says,

[31]*"The blessing of the Lord makes one rich"*

...and I am rich indeed!

My husband proclaiming the
goodness of the Lord!

Princess Lana!

The Family

Chickens for Pets?

When I was young, my dad, although allergic to animals, would feed any stray cat who would knock at our door asking for food. That cat would become our pet and would completely capture my heart.

When I met Al, I discovered that he, too, had a soft spot for animals. So, before children, cats Barnum and Bailey were our "babies." However, after Lana became ill, Dr. Chinnock told us that it would be highly unhealthy for Lana to have a pet.

Chickens, especially, weren't in our plans. UNTIL, one day, my husband called to tell me that someone wanted to give us a couple of chickens. Since we didn't have dinner plans, I figured that chicken would be an ideal main dish to add to the cauliflower that I had in the refrigerator. Al informed me that he was referring to "live" chickens. When he further shared that the animals came with food and a cage, I thought that it would be fun to have chicken eggs. So, even though we knew nothing about caring for chickens, we agreed to take on this project.

When Al brought the animals home, I quickly fell in love *(surprise, surprise!)* and "Rainbow" and "Glory" became our pets. Now, two adorable chickens snuggle on my lap and we eat tasty eggs on a regular basis.

Highlights of my Life and Fun Memories

My husband loves to fish. When we first got married, whenever Al came home with fish, he made a HUGE mess, and since I couldn't stand the smell, taste, or fish pieces that I would find on the counter and floor, this was particularly unpleasant for me.

Over the years, he became more proficient with the "clean-up," except for one particular time: He announced that the kitchen was complete and it was my turn to perform the final "cleaning" test. After being pleasantly surprised to find that the floors, counters, and sink seemed spotless, it was now time to turn on the garbage disposal. I thought it best to first check, so when I put my hand inside the mechanism, I felt something squishy. When I pulled out a fish eye, I screamed, "ALFRED, THE FISH IS LOOKING AT ME!" After being grossed out for a few minutes, I broke into hysterics, and of course, Al joined me.

My son could read before he could talk! He would read the page numbers on the bottom of his books. He loved numbers and he loved money. During one of our Las Vegas trips, Alfie, who was three, ran up to a slot machine, in order to read the sign on the machine which said in big letters, "TWENTY-FIVE CENTS." That year, he spoke his first word, "seven," which he read out loud from the middle of a page in the Bible.

I figured that I would take advantage of his love for money, so, when he was four years old, I offered Alfie twenty dollars to stop sucking his thumb. He never sucked his thumb again. *Maybe I could have gotten away with giving him five bucks instead!*

At five years old, Alfie was adding and subtracting double-digit numbers and reciting multiplication tables. In second grade, he scored in the ninety-ninth percentile on the math section of a nationwide test *(mom's bragging rights!)*.

I always strived to give my kids a fulfilling social life. This was difficult due to recurring medical challenges and hospitalizations, so, whenever possible, Lana and Alfie's friends would spend the night. Since we attended church regularly, whoever was in our home on Sunday mornings would join us.

Awakening kids was a challenge, so, in order to get them up, I would sing the song with the words, "Rise and shine and give God your glory, glory!" and would continue singing until all children were awake and in the "standing position." The longer it took them to get out of bed, the longer they would have to endure the annoying song. *I wonder if any of the kids will someday sing this to their children!*

Alfie taught Sunday school for seven years. To this day, his students still talk about how he was their favorite. He also sang on our church's worship team.

Alfie's friend, Travis, spent many of his younger years with us and it was our pleasure to include him in our activities. Travis would often knock at our front door and say, "I'm home." One time, while Alfie was out of town visiting his cousin, Seth, Travis called to tell Alfie that he was spending the night in Alfie's bed!

When Travis was ten years old, he went to Guatemala on a mission's trip. Since Alfie couldn't go due to our situation with Lana, he wanted to help with the funds needed for Travis. So, Alfie approached friends, family, neighbors, restaurant managers, and everyone else he could think of, and sold almost three hundred See's chocolate bars.

When Lana and Alfie were older, we participated in a home-school bowling league. Lana especially cherished these times, as she was able to be around other families. As she became physically stronger, her bowling greatly improved, and Alfie was a pleasure to watch, as his top score was two hundred fifty-nine!

I love birthdays - and throughout the years, I've had some amazing birthday celebrations! As a child (and even through some adult years), my parents would buy my favorite ice cream cake (mint chip and chocolate chip) and take the family to a lobster dinner. *I miss those times!* One year, they bought tickets for Al and me to see Telly Savalas in "The King and I." Since I was a theatre lover, this was quite a treat - we had great seats, too!

My friend, Ellen, threw me a surprise party at our church's home group. I had never been thrown a party like this, so I was especially touched. Ellen (and others) decorated the fellowship hall, provided a delicious lunch, gifts, and cake, and set up a special table with fancy plates and silverware for me and my family.

My favorite birthday celebration happened years ago when my husband surprised me with front row seats to a Stevie Nicks (young people may not know who she is) concert. At that time, I had the same hair style as Stevie and we looked like we could have been sisters. Al and I were Fleetwood Mac and Stevie Nicks fans, so we sang along with all of the songs!

Since Lana hasn't been able to attend many parties because of her health, we do our best to bring celebrations to her. Every year, we have a "birthday bash" with friends, family, a "Princess" Bounce House, along with chicken, cake, soda, chips (and everything else that goes with those major food groups)!

We used to rent a jump house for Alfie's birthdays, until he and his friends began jumping from our roof into the jump house.

On Lana's eleventh birthday, Alfie and I were [32] baptized in our pool. After learning the importance of this, I was excited. In fact, I was so excited that I forgot to hold my breath and I swallowed a bunch of water.

The following year, on her twelfth birthday, Lana was also baptized in our pool (by her godmother, Ellen), and years later, my husband followed suit. *Great times of celebration!*

In 2014, I went on a mission trip to Israel. I hadn't been on a plane in twenty-two years, so although I was somewhat terrified, I knew I was in God's hands and that this journey was part of His plan for me. I, along with an awesome team, went to places where Jesus walked - like Jerusalem, Bethlehem, and Jericho. We took a boat ride on the Sea of Galilee (where Jesus and His disciples were), placed prayers in the Wailing Wall, and floated on the Dead Sea.

AND … I couldn't miss a once-in-a-lifetime opportunity to follow Jesus' footsteps and be baptized in the Jordan River!

Friends and cousins come together to celebrate
Lana turning twelve

Finding Comfort

For decades, I wondered why I was here and if I had a purpose. I felt unworthy of love and struggled with feelings of never being "good enough."

People came into my life who had an inner peace and an inner strength that I knew could have only come by supernatural means. After talking with them, I found that the common denominator in their stories was Jesus Christ.

Their testimonies brought many questions, so I began searching for the truth. I dove into Bible reading, attended a Biblically based church, received guidance from pastors and rabbis, and prayed that if Jesus was real, He would show me.

I learned from my Bible reading that without the shedding of blood, there could be no atonement for our sins. This is the reason that certain rituals - including the sacrificing of animals - were performed in

Old Testament days. Today, we no longer kill animals (thank goodness!) because Jesus Christ became the "sacrificial lamb." He took the punishment for our sins upon Himself as He chose to give up His life and die on the cross so that we could spend eternity with Him.

> [33]"For this is My blood of the new covenant, which is shed for many for the remission (or forgiveness) of sins."

> [34]"But Christ came as High Priest of the good things that have come, with the greater and more perfect tabernacle not made with hands, that is, not of this creation. Not with the blood of goats and calves, but with His own blood He entered the Most Holy Place once and for all, having obtained eternal redemption."

I realized that the unconditional love and sacrifice of Jesus Christ was the most precious gift that anyone could ever give and that by receiving this gift and asking Him to be Lord of my life, my sins are forgiven. I am guaranteed a place in Heaven, but not because I am a "good person" or by my kind acts, but because of the sacrifice that Jesus made on the cross.

When I chose to follow Jesus, I began to experience a new freedom, confidence, peace, and joy.

The obstacles and challenges in my life became manageable because I knew that He would be with me through them all. So, who is Jesus to me? - He is my provider, comforter, healer, physician, counselor, friend, teacher, mentor, salvation; my peace, hope, joy, miracle worker; my Messiah, and my God.

He is my shelter in the *HEART of the Storm!*

Are God and Jesus Connected?

For many years, I questioned how and if God and Jesus were connected.

Throughout the Old Testament, I found many verses which spoke of the coming Messiah. In the book of Isaiah, the following words were recorded [35] hundreds of years before Jesus Christ came to earth:

[36]*"For unto us a Child is born,*
Unto us a Son is given;
And His name will be called Wonderful,
Counselor, Mighty God,
Everlasting Father,
Prince of Peace."

[37]*"Surely He has borne our sicknesses*
And carried our pains;
But He was wounded for our transgressions,
He was bruised for our iniquities;
We have turned,
every one, to his own way;
And the Lord has laid on Him
the iniquity of us all."

As I continued reading, I became certain that the two testaments were connected. I realized that the Messiah who was spoken about in the Old Testament was revealed in the New Testament to be Jesus Christ.

In the book of Genesis, God spoke about the [38] seed of Abraham coming to the earth and blessing the whole world. *I believe that Jesus is that seed!*

Jesus said:

> [39]*"...if you believed Moses,*
> *you would believe Me,*
> *for he wrote about Me."*

> [40]*"And I give them eternal life,*
> *and they shall never perish;*
> *neither shall anyone snatch them*
> *out of My hand.*
> *My Father, who has given them to Me,*
> *is greater than all;*
> *and no one is able to snatch them*
> *out of My Father's hand.*
> *I and My Father are One."*

> [41]*"I am in My Father, and you in Me,*
> *and I in you."*

According to Messianic Rabbi K.A. Schneider, Old Testament law was the first part of God's grace and then when Jesus came, God's grace was completely revealed.

42"For the law was given through Moses;
grace was realized through Jesus Christ."

43"In the beginning was the Word,
and the Word was with God,
and the Word was God.
He was in the beginning with God."

YES, I was excited to discover that God
and Jesus are most definitely connected!

Can I Be Jewish and Christian at the Same Time?

When I discovered that Jesus and His disciples were Jewish and that the New Testament was written by Jews (inspired by the Holy Spirit), I was ecstatic to learn that - YES - I can be both Jewish and a follower of [44]"Yeshua" at the same time!

I believe that Jesus Christ is the Messiah for Jews and Gentiles alike. He is the Son of man and the Son of God, and is the prophesied fulfillment of the "Tenakh" (or Old Testament).

> [45]*"There is neither Jew nor Greek,*
> *there is neither slave nor free,*
> *there is neither male nor female;*
> *for you are all one in Christ Jesus.*
> *And if you are Christ's,*
> *then you are Abraham's seed, and heirs*
> *according to the promise."*
>
> [46]*"For there is no distinction between*
> *Jew and Greek, for the same Lord over all*
> *is rich to all who call upon Him."*

Why Did I Write This Book?

It all started in 2009 when I spoke at a ladies breakfast at church. At the event, I shared about the miracles that the Lord had done throughout my life and how I came to know Jesus. I spoke about Lana, my marriage, and how, through my relationship with the Lord, I was able to forgive and love again.

After speaking, a few of the ladies came up to me and suggested that I write a book. I thought only one thing: *"It sounds like a lot if work!"*

A few years later, my husband and I spent time with my Uncle Larry (who sadly died during the writing of this book) and Aunt Norma. My aunt had recently written a best-selling book entitled, "Breaking Down the Walls," which tells of her life's struggles and rewards. Since she was aware of some of my story, she was encouraging me to also write a book.

Again, I thought, *"This would be so difficult."*

In the years to follow, I would sense a voice inside gently nudging me to give my testimony. I said, *"Lord, if You want me to write a book, You'll have to help me every step of the way."*

In the Bible, King David spoke about the [47] Lord guiding him (through the [48] Holy Spirit) as he wrote many chapters in the Old Testament. Like David (and other scribes and prophets), the Lord's "spiritual hand" has been upon me, and without Him, I wouldn't have been able to write this book. *I am so grateful!*

My heart's desire is that many, including those in my Jewish family, would come to the realization about who our Messiah is, and that through a relationship with Him, peace and hope would come, even in the midst of life's most challenging storms.

> [49]*"The Lord bless you and keep you;*
> *The Lord make His face shine upon you,*
> *And be gracious to you;*
> *The Lord look upon you with favor,*
> *And give you peace."*

Jill's acting days

Al and Jill - 1998

Lana loves her brother!

Lana hangin' out
-three years old-

Best friends
Lana and Brigitte
1994

Lana blow-drying
grandpa's head

Precious times with
"Mom" (grandma)

Doctor Alfie examines
Officer Lana

Best buddies
Lana and Trisha

Proud mommy and her children - 1996

Alfie and Lana - 1999

Family party for Lana's fourteenth birthday

"Mom" and "Dad" are so proud of
their granddaughter!

Lana and Uncle Devin

Grandma Jackie, Lana, Jill and Alfie

Best dance ever -
with grandpa!

Food Pantry ministry team (partial)

"Grandpa" Alan

About the Author

Jill H. Loera was born in New York and raised in a Jewish community in Long Island. At a young age, she and her family moved to North Hollywood, California. After receiving a Bachelor of Arts Degree in Theatre Arts at Cal State University Northridge, she worked within the entertainment industry while pursuing an acting career. Twelve years later, the author turned in her scripts, married her husband, and had two children.

Shortly after, Jill became a Christian and she and her family joined the church at Rancho Christian Center. Eighteen years later, Jill runs the church's Food Pantry and is involved in a variety of church ministries.

The author is blessed to be married to her husband of thirty years. They have resided in their Upland home for nearly two decades, along with their daughter and two pet chickens. Their son lives close-by and has frequent visits with the family.

I met the author Jill Loera nearly twenty years ago when on assignment as a tutor for her daughter Lana. Since I was in the family's home a few times a week, a relationship began to develop. I was becoming drawn in with fascination and admiration. The family's circumstances appeared insurmountable, yet they exuded optimism, hope and joy; negativity had no place in their lives. After my assignment ended, a strong friendship with Jill, her husband Al, and their children Lana and Alfie, ensued. Today, we are like family.

Jill is a genuine, loving, bright, spiritual woman who is a precious gift, so when she asked if I would help to edit her book, I was deeply touched.

When I read *Heart of the Storm* for the first time, I was gripped with emotion as I turned from one page to the next. It became clear that I would not be editing during my first read. I was amazed by the family's perseverance and their love and strength to withstand seemingly endless adversity.

This book is a poignant testimony of how the author continues to find shelter and hope in the midst of extreme challenges.

With splashes of humor, Jill takes us through a rich journey of her life's disappointments and triumphs and how, through supernatural experiences, darkness and depression are transformed into hope and freedom.

Heart of the Storm has brought me into a heightened sense of priorities and spiritual purpose. I recommend this story to people of all faiths who seek the same.

Sally R. Wachtel
Co-Editor

Author Acknowledgments

I am grateful and blessed to have the love and support of my husband, Al, daughter, Lana, and son, Alfie, whose tremendous insight has helped to guide the course of this book.

Heart of the Storm is dedicated to: My dad, Ron, my brother, Devin, his wife, Patricia, and the rest of the family, including aunts, uncles, and cousins … and in loving memory of Uncle Shelly, Uncle Larry, Marlene, and Patrick, who all passed away during the writing of the book. Thank you, each one, for your inspiration and your love.

I'm also dedicating this book to my mom, Sheila, and to my grandparents, Nana Dorothy, Papa Sol, Nana Lylla, and Papa Jack - all of whom I miss dearly and all of whom had a huge influence on my life.

I am so grateful for the doctors, nurses, technicians, staff, and heart transplant coordinators at Children's Hospital Los Angeles and Loma Linda University Medical Center who have given our family such love and support for many years.

A heartfelt gratitude goes to: The late Dr. Arno Hohn Sr. from Children's Hospital Los

Angeles for saving our little girl's life; Dr. Leonard Bailey from Loma Linda's Heart Center for performing the first successful heart transplant; Dr. Richard Chinnock, who was Lana's doctor for over twenty years and saved her life on more than one occasion; Dr. Steven Gundry and Dr. Anees Razzouk for performing both of Lana's heart transplants; Dr. Liesl Mathias for overseeing Lana's cancer care; Dr. Tamara Shankel and Dr. Liset Stoletniy for being Lana's heart transplant doctors; Dr. Robert Tan, and Dr. Charles Stewart, III for providing Lana with the BEST care.

Also, thank you to the Ronald McDonald House who housed us while we were going through difficult times.

I am forever indebted to my pastors and church family at Rancho Christian Center who continue to love, support, and pray for my family and me.

Thank you to the dear friends who have added such joy to my life. *You know who you are!* And, in loving memory of my sweet friend, Cheryl Proulx.

Words cannot begin to express the gratitude I have for Ellen Miller who has been a part of our family during the last eighteen years of roller-coaster up's and down's. She has been my friend and mentor and has blessed me with her tender heart to serve and love others.

I am especially grateful to Sally Wachtel for her friendship and for her invaluable assistance in helping to edit this book. Her creative brain and willingness to read, re-read, and read still again - without complaining - has been a blessing for me. I will always remember the endless hours spent at Paradise Buffet amidst the delicious food and coffee (especially the Cappuccino Ice Cream) - with papers, pencils, and erasers spread everywhere. What a priceless friend I have in "Sally-Wally!"

Whenever my son, Alfie, would read parts of the book, he would say, "Mom, it's boring." I would reply, "Not again" - and back to the drawing board I would go! I know that because of Alfie, the book is more interesting and I am so grateful!

I also must thank my friend, Deborah Inda (who I and others refer to as my "sister"), who suggested that certain details be added in order to enrich the book's quality. Thank you, sis!

Also, thank you to my friend Steven J. Rich for guiding and encouraging me through many months of writing, editing, designing, and praying! Thank you, also, to his lovely goddaughter, Jeanette Rodriguez who, by Divine appointment, connected Steven and me.

A special thank you to my friend and graphic designer, Marianne Aguilar, for coming in at the "bottom of the ninth" (baseball term) to help with every area of the book, including cover design, book formatting, images, and the final edit. Also, thank you to Bella, her cat, who entertained us by talking to a fly while we worked.

Thank you to my publisher, Jim Bryson, of Spring Mill Publishing, who provided much needed counsel and encouragement.

I was certain that nothing could be more challenging than writing a book UNTIL I realized that "modern" technology would need to play a significant role. If it weren't for the outstanding technical support of: Marianne Aguilar, Levi Miller, Frank Ellis, Kristie Vargas, Alfie Loera, Eric Sheather, Layssa Castleton, and Long Le, photos and other graphics would not be included in this book.

To everyone who is reading this, thank you for allowing me to share my testimony. I pray that this story encourages you and that you allow the Lord to touch you in a way that only He can.

Most of all, thank you to my Heavenly Father, and to Jesus Christ, for inspiring me to share my story, and for teaching me how to live peacefully in the midst of life's storms.

Footnotes

1 Leviticus 16:29-30

2 Psalm 3:3-4

3 Psalm 28:2

4 Isaiah 41:10

5 Numbers 6:24-26

6 John 3:16

7 John 11:25-26

8 Temporary home for families of critically ill children who are hospitalized at Loma Linda Medical Center

9 James 4:8

10 Jeremiah 29:11-13

11 1 John 1:9

12 Isaiah 53:6, Joel 2:32, John 1:29; 14:6, Acts 2:21; 4:12, Romans 10:13, 1 Corinthians 15:3, Ephesians 2:8-9, 1 John 1:7; 2:2; 5:10-12

13 Romans 10:9

14 2 Corinthians 5:17

15 John 5:24

16 John 6:47

17 Matthew 11:28

18 John 14:27

19 Matthew 19:26

20 Merriam-Webster's definition of "enable": A person who facilitates the self-destruction behavior of another.

21 Exodus 34:28, Deuteronomy 9:9, Esther 4:16, Ezra 7:6, 12, 21; 8:21, 23; 10:6, Nehemiah 1:4-11, Daniel 6:18; 9:3, Isaiah 58:6-9, Jeremiah 36:6, 9, Joel 1:14; 2:12-15, Zechariah 7:5, Matthew 17:18-21, Mark 9:29, Luke 4:2, Acts 10:30; 13:2-3

22 1 Kings 8:33-52, Matthew 18:21-22, Mark 11:25-26, Colossians 3:13

23 Jeremiah 33:3, John 14:10-17, 20, 26, John 15:26; 16:7-13, Romans 8:26, 1 Corinthians 2:10-13

24 Deuteronomy 4:29

25 John 5:24, 2 Peter 3:9

26 Romans 14:8

27 "Need You Now" - sung by Plumb

28 "While I'm Waiting" - sung by John Waller

29 The charter school through which we home-schooled

30 Colossians 3:17

31 Proverbs 10:22

32 Matthew 28:19, Mark 1:9-11, Acts 19:6, Romans 6:3-6

33 Matthew 26:28

34 Hebrews 9:11-12

35 Isaiah 53:1; 42:1-9, Zechariah 9:9-10, John 12:14

36 Isaiah 9:6

37 Isaiah 53:4-6

38 Genesis 22:18

39 John 5:46

40 John 10:10, 28-30

41 John 14:20

42 John 1:17

43 John 1:1-2

44 "Yeshua:" 'Salvation' in Hebrew

45 Galatians 3:28

46 Romans 10:12

47 1 Chronicles 28:19

48 John 14:10-17, 20, 26; 15:26; 16:7-13

49 Numbers 6:24-26

Recommended Reading

These anointed books have so enriched my life:

Fruchtenbaum, Arnold. *Jesus Was A Jew.* Tennessee: Broadman Press, 1974

Glaser, Mitch. *Isaiah 53 Explained.* USA: Chosen People Productions, 2010

Rich, Steven J. *Precious Gems From Potter's Clay...Daily Reflections for Quiet Time.* California: Pointe Media, 2012

Rosen, Moishe and Ceil. *Witnessing to Jews.* California: Library of Congress Cataloging-Publication Data, 1998

Telchin, Stan. *Betrayed!* Michigan: Zondervan Publishing House, 1981